2021:
The Year in Leadership

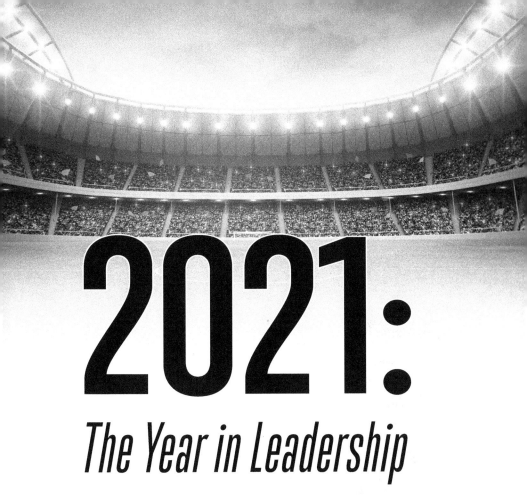

2021:

The Year in Leadership

The Stories of Faith, Athletics, Business,
and Life Which Inspired Us All

BRIAN DODD

XULON PRESS

Xulon Press
2301 Lucien Way #415
Maitland, FL 32751
407.339.4217
www.xulonpress.com

Paperback ISBN-13: 978-1-6628-4354-9
eBook ISBN-13: 978-1-6628-4355-6

Dedicated to Pastors Dr. Crawford Loritts, Dr. Ike Reighard, Mark Marshall, and Mike Linch. God used these four men to help forge me into the leader I am today and continue to become in the days and years ahead.

Praise for Brian Dodd and *2021: The Year in Leadership*

"Brian Dodd is a man of character, a seasoned leader, and has one of the best leadership minds I know. Just a short visit to his website will give quick affirmation of his amazing leadership content. In his new book, *2021- The Year In Leadership: The Stories of Faith, Athletics, Business, and Life Which Inspired Us All;* is nearly encyclopedic in nature with over 80 articles jam-packed with wisdom, practical guidance and inspiring stories that will help you be a better leader today."

Dan Reiland, Executive Pastor
12Stone Church, Lawrenceville
GA. Author of *Confident Leader!*

"Brian's insight and leadership are a trusted voice and valuable guide in my life. His perspective on 2021 will improve your 2022!"

Rusty George Pastor
Author and host of the *Leading Simple Podcast*

"I have had the privilege of calling Brian Dodd a friend for almost 25 years. One thing has proven true through all of those years and that is Brian Dodd always leaves me *better* than when he found me. Whether it is his amazing blog, incredible books or just a lunch to pick his brain, Brian will always take good and make it better! His ability to glean insights from everyday life & even athletics and apply leadership principles to them is incredibly unique! Who wins . . . . . . we all do! If you open this book and read, I promise you will be *better* too!"

Mike Linch
Senior Pastor NorthStar Church
Host of the *Linch with a Leader Podcast*

"Brian Dodd is a unique and inspiring writer, and his articles and topics are unlike most online bloggers today. Brian's focus is leadership and change. His daily blog adds value and empowerment to our daily lives. Brian's articles are also informative, and Brian also writes leadership principles from the movie screen. Many of the movie reviews from Brian have provided me with needed insight. I recommend that you subscribe to Brian's daily blog and purchase his new book, *2021- The Year In Leadership: The Stories of Faith, Athletics, Business, and Life Which Inspired Us All.* You will gain great value from Brian's keen insight and wisdom."

Thomas McDaniels
Senior Pastor of Lifebridge.tv

"One of my favorite leadership quotes is John Maxwell's 'Everything rises and falls on leadership.' At the core, this describes Brian Dodd. Brian's character, conduct and integrity are second to none, and these three characteristics are priorities that drive his life, influence and ministry as a leader. Brian exemplifies focus, passion and discipline, and after spending time with him personally, or when reading his leadership material on his website, I always walk away being better equipped and prepared to face the challenges of leadership."

Kevin Burrell
Major League Baseball Area Scouting Supervisor
of the Chicago White Sox

"I've known Brian for several years. He is one the most integrous and wise leaders I know. Each week he consistently delivers quality, practical posts on leadership. His site is 'THE' leadership source I go to for the best of the best curated leadership insight. He is a top leadership docent every leader should follow and learn from."

Dr. Charles Stone
Lead Pastor of West Park Church

"The reader who wants to get an emersion in leadership theory and practice can start with Brian Dodd. Regardless of your professional focus—business, sports, spiritual, etc.—his work can touch your mind and your heart. Brian's website, "Brian Dodd on Leadership." is rich with the best in contemporary material. His book *Timeless* is an outstanding treatment of "Apex Leaders." His combination of both leadership quotes and leadership examples is, in my judgement, without parallel. But what really sets him apart is his practice of developing spiritual leaders through his consulting and writing on church strategy and growth. Place his latest book at the top of your personal development plans for 2022."

George Manners
Emeritus Professor
Kennesaw State University

"Brian Dodd is a leader who has worked and interfaced with leaders from across the country for over two decades. He possesses that quality leaders must possess . . . he himself is a learner. And he shares what he is learning. He learns from the best and shares the best of what he learns from them and his own experiences. In his new book, *2021-The Year of Leadership: The Stories of Faith, Athletics, Business, and Life Which Inspired Us All,* he shares inspirational, relevant, and leadership lessons from his 2021 posts. Can't wait to get it! Thank you Brian."

Claude Thomas
Pastor Emeritus
Keystone Church

"Imagine a leader who helps other leaders be the best leaders they can be; that is Brian Dodd. Leadership lessons are everywhere and Brian Dodd is gifted and specializes in finding them or pointing them out. You can find these lessons each week on his website, which is one of the top leadership sites in the world. He lives to encourage others and churches to be all that God has called them to be. There is no one better at promoting and lifting up others.

As someone who is privileged to personally call him a friend, I have come to realize everybody needs a Brian Dodd in their life!"

Nate Galloway
Family Ministries Pastor
Piedmont Church

"As leaders we are always looking for information to help us improve. But how do you sort through it in these days of information overload? What if you had someone who would find and deliver the best of that information to you in a single place? Well, Brian Dodd is that person, and briandoddonleadership.com is the place. As a prolific writer, researcher, and great leader himself, Brian is offering up the best of the best from his writings over the past year. As a leader, his newest book, *2021—The Year in Leadership: The Stories of Faith, Athletics, Business, and Life Which Inspired Us All* is a must have."

Mark Marshall
Assistant Executive Director
Georgia Baptist Mission Board

"Brian Dodd is one of the most diligent researchers and students of leadership I've ever met. He does a great service for all of us who want to improve our people and leadership skills, because he's always looking for the best, proven illustrations of great leadership practices. This latest book is indicative of his passion to help us learn from the best. Blended with Brian's interest in total person development . . . professional, soul and spiritual . . . it's another powerful tool for leaders and those who desire to effectively serve others."

Steve Robinson
Former CMO of Chick-fil-A
Author of *Covert Cows and Chick-fil-A*

"Brian Dodd is truly one of the best writers I know on the subject of leadership. His content is always solid gold. This work is no exception. This will inspire you and challenge you to your core. Thanks for another great work, Brian!"

Shawn Lovejoy
Founder/CEO of Courage To Lead

"With the vast numbers of leaders profiled and the issues they faced in 2021 you will not face an issue in 2022 that these leaders have not already solved in the covers of this exciting new book by Brian Dodd! Brian Dodd is my go-to guy with his blog which is one of the top 25 blogs in the world on leadership. You will find no one better at extracting nuggets of solid gold from leaders in every sphere of life . . . Brian has assembled the wisdom and insights from those at high levels of influence and this book gives you unfettered access to the best of their thinking!"

Dr. Dwight "Ike" Reighard
President/CEO MUST Ministries
Senior Pastor Piedmont Church

"According to Inc. Magazine, Brian Dodd is a 'Top 100 Speaker on Leadership,' and I agree. However, I believe Brian is #1 and unrivaled at breaking down real leadership content real-time in a clear, consistent, and constant fashion. As leaders, it is one thing to pick your learning environment—it is another thing when your learning environment picks you. We are the true benefactors of the leadership environments that select Brian—which is why I go to BrianDoddOnLeadership.com daily to consume leadership."

Jason Stoughton
The John Maxwell Company

"I am always amazed in my heart and mind concerning the principles of leadership Brian Dodd extracts from everyday experiences. His giftedness of connecting life situations and circumstances to leadership paradigms compels me to read *2021—The Year in Leadership: The Stories of Faith, Athletics, Business, and Life Which Inspired Us All.* Just as his blogs and previous books have enhanced my ability to lead and teach leadership to others, his newest delivery will challenge our lives for 2022."

Marty Benton
President of Vision Street Ministries

"Simple. Inspiring. Practical. Brian Dodd has put together a 'leadership library' to grow your leadership capacity no matter what your profession is. If there is only one book you read this year, read this one and learn from one of the best!"

Daniel Lucas
Lead Pastor of Better Life Church

Table of Contents

Introduction

Leadership is more difficult than it has ever been. There is more ambiguity than there has ever been, and a lot less clarity. People are also more broken than ever before. They are scared. Anxiety is a constant unwelcome companion for so many when they awake in the morning. It seems there is no need to make plans. Everything will soon be upended. Relationships have been damaged over masks, social distancing, vaccines, Zoom, and yes, even toilet paper.

When will the madness that began in 2020 end? The truth is no one knows. But what we do know is everything truly does rise and fall with leadership. Leaders are needed now more than ever. This is why Brian Dodd On Leadership (www.briandoddonleadership.com) exists, and the book *2021 The Year in Leadership: The Stories of Faith, Athletic, Business, and Life Which Inspired Us All* was written. Throughout 2021, I consistently brought content and lessons to help leaders navigate these uncertain waters. The following pages are a chronological look at my most impactful posts throughout the year.

Let me tell you what you will read. Each chapter is a post from 2021, starting in January with the college football play-offs. You will have the opportunity to learn today from what was a real-time event at the time of writing. The content contains the greatest lessons from business, sports, family, nonprofits, and Christianity I had the privilege of witnessing last year. The book does not have to be read in order. If you see chapters about leaders or events that interest you from the table of contents, you can jump straight to them. Many are slightly edited from the original posts for better reading. The lessons from the following pages were timely, relevant, and simply made leaders better. And they will do the same for you even today.

Let me also tell you what you will not read. I will not address presidential elections, insurrections, racial unrest, or pandemics. I will leave that to other "experts" who seemingly do nothing but divide audiences.

This book would not be possible without the readers who makes up the Brian Dodd On Leadership (BDL) audience. Their loyalty has birthed a popular website, two previous leadership books, a podcast, and most recently, a coaching course. If you are not part of the BDL leadership tribe, then following pages are especially for you. It's time to get better as a leader. Let's get to work!

January 1–The Courageous Leadership of Justin Fields

With 5:57 remaining in the second quarter of the Ohio State Buckeyes–Clemson Tigers College Football Playoff semifinal game, Ohio State quarterback Justin Fields left the safety of the pocket and scrambled down the middle of the field. It was there where he received a wicked hit to the ribs from Clemson linebacker James Skalski. After lying on the ground and writhing in pain for several moments, Fields was helped off the field. After missing just one play, Fields returned to the game. Despite being in enormous pain and holding his injured ribs, Fields immediately threw a nine-yard touchdown pass to wide receiver Chris Olave. Fields would go on to finish the game completing twenty-two of twenty-eight passes for 385 yards and a Sugar Bowl record six touchdowns. What makes leadership courageous is its willingness to pay the heavy price needed to overcome significant adversity.

Fields admitted to ESPN's Tom Rinaldi afterwards, "That hit really took a toil on me. My ribs were killing me pretty much all game." He also said in the postgame press conference he could not run and that every pass he threw hurt. Oftentimes, leaders need assistance during challenging times. From a physical standpoint, Fields acknowledged needing "a couple shots" while in the medical tent after the Skalski's hit. But what inspired him the most was not something physical, it was something emotional. Fields admitted to Rinaldi, "What pushed me through was the love for my brothers. I would do anything for these guys." Courageous leadership is often driven by love. It is the feeling that I can't let my friends down.

Buckeyes head coach Ryan Day seemed particularly inspired by Fields's courage. He said in an ESPN postgame interview, "He took a big hit. He looked me in the eye and said, 'There's no way we're losing this game.'" Fields was correct. The Buckeyes defeated the Tigers 49–28. Day summed up what we all feel about courageous leaders. He said, "What he means to me I can't put into words. . . . What a tough and special young man Justin Fields is."

Courageous leaders are tough, special, and cannot be put into words.

January 4–Black Monday

All leadership is temporary. Sadly, few leaders ever get to leave their positions of influence on their own terms. Oftentimes, they are removed prior to their desired time of transition. Perhaps you can relate.

January 4 was known as Black Monday in the National Football League. Traditionally it is the first day after the season's conclusion, and many coaches and general managers are fired by their teams. But they are not the only ones affected by this stark reality. Many players also know they have played their last down for their current teams as well. Such appeared to be the case for tight end Zach Ertz of the Philadelphia Eagles. Ertz had played for the team each of his eight seasons in the league. He was a three-time Pro Bowler and caught the winning score in the Eagles' Super Bowl LII victory over the New England Patriots. Ertz is a great player, but it appeared his time as an Eagle had concluded.

After the team's loss to the Washington Football Team, Ertz sat on the bench alone for several moments, contemplating all the events taking place both that day and throughout his career. As mentioned earlier, all leadership assignments eventually come to an end.

They are temporary. We must follow Ertz's example and steward it well while we have it. Ertz said in a post-game news conference, "This city is the best city to play for. I couldn't have asked for a better experience." And, the city of Philadelphia couldn't have asked for a better experience than watching Zach Ertz play.

January 6–Going Too Fast

Jeff Martin is the lead pastor of Redeemer Community Church in Johnson City, Tennessee. He told me a story from his days as a youth pastor in San Antonio. Jeff had developed a great relationship with the local high school basketball coach. However, this was not just any coach. This coach led one of Texas's annual powerhouse programs which regularly competed for and won state championships. Jeff and this coach were sitting together one day, watching the middle-school boys play. This was a unique experience because this was the feeder system for the high school program. The coach would one day be leading many of these players and already knew each of their names and tendencies.

The team played an up-tempo style and full court pressed the entire game. Their constant pressure overwhelmed the other team as they built up an insurmountable lead. Expecting the coach to be excited about the future, Jeff asked what his thoughts were. His answer was quite surprising. He disgustedly said, "This is fool's gold." Surprised, Jeff asked why. The coach went on to explain that playing fast was teaching him nothing about these players. The coach wished that the team would simply play some form of standard defense. Playing a standard defense would teach the players to identify different opposing offenses and setup better. He said, "The scoreboard is fool's gold if you're not setting up for the future. Don't always run a full court press. Slow down for the long haul."

As Jeff, who is about to turn thirty-six years old, was telling me this story, he said, "Brian, what got me to thirty-six won't get me to forty-six." What Jeff was implying was, do not confuse movement with progress. Going fast as a leader creates a lot of activity but may not produce long-term results. Also, short-term results produced by speed may be a false indicator of lack of true talent. Speed often competes with wisdom and intelligence. As the coach said, going too fast may prevent you from developing the ability to accurately process the environment you are in and situation you are facing. To avoid unnecessary confusion, you need to slow down and set aside time for contemplation.

January 11–Coach Nick Saban

One person who obviously spends a great deal of time contemplating is Alabama Crimson Tide head coach Nick Saban. Is it me, or did he seem like he was having fun following his team's 52–24 demolition of Ohio State in the 2021 national championship game? Afterward, he had a very insightful interview with ESPN's Scott Van Pelt. Regarding the challenges faced by COVID during the regular season, he said, "The team that handles the disruptions the best is the team that's going to have the best chance to be successful in the end." He went on to elaborate by adding, "A lot of the disruptions . . . actually made the team closer and we became a better team because of some of the disruptions . . . When something gets taken away from you, we all have more appreciation for it when we get it back."

Coach Saban then went on to praise offensive coordinator Steve Sarkisian for his commitment to the program, leading up to the championship game. You see, Sarkisian was in great demand after the team's record-setting year and could have been easily distracted by his many head-coaching opportunities. He would eventually accept the job at the University of Texas Longhorns. Saban said,

"Some people would have a difficult time taking the head-coaching job at Texas the day or two after we beat Notre Dame and staying focused on what they needed to do. But that shows his appreciation for the players. That's something I really admire in him." Coach Saban added, "I think that's the most important thing in being a coach. You care about the players. You want to do what's best for the players." The man affectionally known as "Sark" did just that.

But what Coach Saban said which had the greatest impact was on the concept of the University of Alabama Crimson Tide football program creating value for its student-athletes. He said, "I have a lot of pride in performance and want to do the best I possibly can as a coach to have the best program that creates value for the players. I'm talking about value in terms of personal development, academics, and graduating and developing and careers off the field, career development, and as football players . . . That's why we get a lot of good players." Let's recap that final statement. There are five areas the Alabama program adds value to its players:

1. Personal Development
2. Academics
3. Graduating
4. Developing a Career off the Field
5. Developing a Career on the Field as a Professional Football Player

As leaders, how is your program developing those serving on your team?

January 15–*WandaVision*

Today was the release of the Marvel Cinematic Universe's first Disney+ series *WandaVision*. Let's be honest, I did not know what to expect. The previews showed a version of Wanda Maximoff (played by Elizabeth Olsen) and Vision (played by Paul Bettany) in some '50s combination of *Leave It to Beaver* and *I Dream of Jeanie*. My expectation of any Marvel production is big action, great storytelling, bad guys, and some threat of global destruction. Before Wanda became the most interesting character in the Marvel Universe by the series end, I was incredibly disappointed in the first two episodes. The storyline was Wanda and Vision are in some form of alternate highly domesticated universe, trying to have a normal life and just fit in. But something seems awry.

First let me give some over-arching leadership thoughts: trust is the foundation of all successful relationships. I trust Kevin Feige and the Marvel films. Therefore, I was willing to give this some time. Also, you should always take the time needed to develop a proper perspective. There was enough in the first two episodes (particularly at the end of the second) which would keep me engaged moving forward. This storyline was going somewhere, and I found myself interested in seeing where it was.

As the series unfolded, *WandaVision* became a case study in how someone handles grief. Elizabeth Olsen's portrayal of a young woman who had tragically lost the love of her life (Vision), as well as her brother, and the extraordinary means she went through to cope with the pain was riveting. I trusted Feige and the Marvel franchise. My trust was rewarded. I can't wait to see where Marvel goes with the Scarlet Witch character.

January 17—Andy Reid's Courageous Decision

There comes a time in every leader's life when he or she must make a courageous decision. The stakes are high, and a leader's mettle is tested. The decision made could bring great glory to the leader and success to their team *or*, conversely, great pain and disappointment. Courageous decisions are defining moments for a leader. Such an event happened during the Kansas City Chiefs and Cleveland Browns play-off game. The defending Super Bowl champion Chiefs were without superstar quarterback Patrick Mahomes who was injured earlier in the game. With only one minute, twenty-five seconds remaining in the game and clinging to a five-point lead, head coach Andy Reid was faced with a critical decision. On fourth down and one, should he try to draw the Browns offside and punt, leaving the game in the hands of his defense—or should he try to put the game away with a first down? Conventional wisdom said to punt.

To the surprise of many, back-up quarterback Chad Henne threw a pass to wide receiver Tyreek Hill for a first down. CBS broadcaster Tony Romo understood the magnitude of Coach Reid's decision. He loudly proclaimed, "Only Andy Reid gets in the shotgun on fourth-and-one and throws the ball!"

Afterward, a victorious Reid held a post-game news conference. If you closely read his words, you can deconstruct the anatomy of a courageous decision:

1. Rely on your experience when making courageous decisions: "I'm glad he (back-up quarterback Chad Henne) had an opportunity to play a week or two ago . . . I think that helped him when he jumped in this time being comfortable with the speed of everything."
2. Prepare or repair. Courageous decisions should be made in advance: "We go through those on Saturday nights, situations to win the game. 4th and 1 . . . what do you want?"
3. Making courageous decisions is a collaborative process: "My coaches were on board."

4. Stay positive when making courageous decisions: "Nobody got down. Nobody was hanging their head or moping in the game . . . Those guys kept battling."

5. Courageous decisions are only made by courageous leaders: "Somewhere you got to reach deep during the tough times and pull that out."

6. Don't flinch when making courageous decisions: "If the coaches are flinching, it's not going to happen. The locker room is not going to flinch."

7. Confidence exceeds doubt when making courageous decisions: "It builds confidence in the coaches. There was no doubt. There was no doubt we were going to go for it and go for that play."

8. Leaders should boldly communicate courageous decisions: "Hey, there's no tomorrow. Let's go. Let's roll."

9. Courageous decisions require extra effort from everyone on your team: "Everybody just pick your game up an inch, and let's go."

10. Courageous decisions require unity and alignment: "Have a play ready to go everyone likes. There's no flinching."

11. There is often no time to evaluate courageous decisions.: "There's no time to say anything other than 'Let's go.' You're trying to win the game. There's no time. You've rehearsed that before. There's not time to talk about it."

12. You only make courageous decisions when respecting those who carry out the decisions: "That's the part that I think is a tribute to Chad. The way he handles himself. You don't earn that respect from the coaches and players without handling yourself the right way every day . . . No one had any doubt."

Just to recap, the following provides the framework and decision-grid for courageous decisions based upon Coach Reid's comments:

1. Rely on your experience;
2. Prepare;
3. Collaborate with your leaders;
4. Be positive;
5. Be courageous yourself;
6. Don't flinch;
7. Be confident;
8. Boldly communicate the decision;
9. Ask for more from your team;
10. Be unified;
11. Only then you can take action;
12. But only take action with people you respect.

February 7—Tom Brady and the Finish Line

Leadership is an oval track. What do I mean by this statement? I simply mean there is no finish line. There's only what's next, what's ahead. As Super Bowl LV approached, Tampa Bay Buccaneer's legendary quarterback said in the game's hype video, "In this journey there is no final destination. There's only the next one." There is so much embedded in Tom's words. Since there is no final destination here on Earth, what counts is the journey itself and the opportunities provided along the way. As a result, those moments require focus, preparation, and the commitment to seize them.

Many leaders relax or become complacent. They rest on yesterday's success. We must challenge ourselves daily and be committed to personal growth. I once had a supervisor continually remind me to "quit reading my newspaper clippings." In other words, it was what was ahead that counted. Keep growing. Keep challenging yourself. Keep learning. Learn from Tom Brady: No matter what you've accomplished, there are still games left to play.

February 12–Trevor Lawrence's Pro Day

From legendary champion Tom Brady, we will shift to the supposed next big thing: Trevor Lawrence. Today the Clemson Tigers quarterback's pro day was telecast on ESPN2. This was quite an extraordinary event. Because of an upcoming surgery on his non-throwing shoulder, he moved this workout up five to six weeks to accommodate the teams interested in his services. This limited his preparation time with quarterback coach Jordan Palmer and the receivers who would participate with him. But it did not matter. While there may be many teams wanting to draft him, he will not get by the Jacksonville Jaguars who have the first overall pick. In fact, new head coach Urban Meyer was only several yards from Lawrence the entire workout.

Of all the comments made by the ESPN's analysts during the broadcast, the one which made the largest impact on me was from E.J. Manuel. He said, "The most important thing is for him to understand what they're bringing him in to be. They're not bringing him in there to be polite, to be the nice guy. You're the number one pick, and they're building this team and franchise around you. You're part CEO of this franchise. For him, it's a matter of speaking up . . . They're expecting you to come in and win . . . Earn that leadership role by working hard and doing what you need to do in practice and showing up on time. Be early and the last guy out, take that command from day one."

There is so much to digest from Manuel's comments. Primary is the self-awareness leaders must have. I'm not referring to personality traits but rather an understanding of the responsibility which comes with the leadership position. The franchise is building its team and culture around you. As the leader, you must speak up, and your team must produce positive results. Passivity and low production are not your friends. You must also understand that what got you into the room are your previous accomplishments. But what will keep you in the room and earn respect is what you do moving forward. It is a sobering reality that "real recognizes real." Those you lead will know if you have what it takes or not, probably long before those you report to.

As the leader, you will set the tone for the entire organization. You must show up first and leave last. In addition, you must be your team's hardest worker. Everyone wants the leadership perks, but few are willing to pay the accompanying price. Most of all, you must show consistency by doing these things each and every single day over and over and over again. Faithfulness and consistency must become your leadership brand. What you do every day must become what people think about when you walk in a room or connect with them.

This is what Trevor Lawrence is signing up for as a leader. More important, it's what you signed up for as well.

February 14—What Pastors Gave Us During 2020 and COVID

Today I had the privilege of speaking at a local luncheon honoring pastors in our area. After much prayer and thought, I wanted to express to those in attendance I was aware of the incredible challenges and hardships they faced during 2020. In addition to acknowledging their reality, I wanted to remind each of the value they provided to so many during one of the darkest periods of their lives.

The following was the content of my speech entitled "*Seven Things Pastors Gave Us During 2020 and COVID.*"

Pastors Gave Us Safety

Pastors and their staffs overly communicated and managed service times, parking instructions, gathering locations, traffic flow, restrooms, off-limits locations, mask policies, seating requirements for social distancing, disinfectant usage, and exiting instructions. No details were left out. Because of this, I agree with retired First Baptist Church of Woodstock, Georgia, pastor Johnny Hunt who said, "There's not a safer place to be than a church on Sunday morning."

Pastors Gave Us Dignity

As church attenders and members, we needed a shepherd in 2020 more than ever before. Because every pastor was now leading a small or mid-sized church in attendance, they got to know almost all our names and stories. As a result, our opinions were valued. We were noticed and felt like we mattered. Pastors, if it's possible, you actually made us feel at home during the pandemic.

Pastors Gave Us a Model for Creativity and Handling Change

- They had to learn to preach both to and through a camera. This speaks to learning new communication skills.
- They had to conduct weddings and funerals differently. This speaks to learning to administer care differently.
- They had to conduct outdoor services and preach to people in cars. This speaks to overcoming barriers and providing creative solutions.
- They learned about the Payroll Protection Plan. This speaks to learning new administrative and banking skills.
- They had to lead their staffs differently. This speaks to becoming better leaders.
- They had to make more hard decisions than ever. This speaks to their courage.

- Many of them, along with their wives, had to learn to become homeschool parents. This speaks to leading their families in new ways.
- They had to become Zoom experts. This speaks to their ability to learn technological skills.
- They received countless amounts of criticism over race, politics, masks, opening dates, closing dates, and even more from church members, people in the community, social media, their staffs, and yes, even members of their own families. Pastors learned how much resilience they really had.

Pastors Gave Us Stability

In the midst of unprecedented change and uncertainty, many pastors remained focused on their mission, vision, and core values. People still got saved and baptized during 2020. Regardless of the times you live in, it is all about disciple-making and life-change.

Pastors Gave Us What Is Most Vital—The Word of God

This is the most important of the seven points listed. Many pastors taught us how to process the events of 2020 through a biblical worldview. We were all reminded the Bible is the greatest leadership book ever written and does the following:

- The Bible provides reassurance during unstable times;
- The Bible elevates our thinking;
- The Bible teaches us righteous living in times of lawlessness;
- The Bible is used by the Holy Spirit to convict us of our sins;
- The Bible challenges us to repent and do better;
- The Bible calls for a decision. The year 2020 was not a time for passivity or sitting on the fence. Many issues forced Christians to take a stand; and
- The Bible provides clear next steps once decisions are made.

Pastors Gave Us Hope

Pastors told us that we could make it. It is a fundamental leadership truth that leaders point to a brighter tomorrow. They are dealers of hope. Think about it, if you are not pointing to a brighter future, why would I or anyone else follow you into it? Pastors were one of the only constant sources of encouragement during 2020.

Pastors Gave Us Something Extraordinary

The difference between ordinary and extraordinary is just a little extra. The follow are just some of the little extra things pastors did during 2020:

- Pastors gave us extra prayers;
- Pastors made extra phone calls to their members;
- Pastors conducted and attended extra meetings;
- Pastors showed extra grace when they were given countless "suggestions";
- Pastors showed extra compassion to sick and hurting people;
- Pastors preached extra Sunday morning sermons;
- Pastors made extra visits to senior adult homes and kept them connected;
- Pastors took advantages of extra opportunities to serve their communities;
- Pastors took extra time to equip their staffs and leaders for a new and uncertain reality;
- Pastors showed extra love to their families;
- Pastors did extra learning because new leadership skills were required; and
- Pastors had extra resilience during 2020 and kept showing up for work week after week after week.

Pastors were simply extraordinary during 2020, and we are all better people for it.

It's been said that when Jesus is all you have, you will find Jesus is all you need. I am sure that is the case. But I do not want to imagine a world where we do not have pastors.

February 21–Handling Tragedy and Setbacks

Alex Zanardi is a living legend. Born in Italy in 1966, Zanardi grew up racing. His Formula 1 debut took place at the 1991 Spanish Grand Prix. After modest success in Europe, he came to America in 1995 and began working for Champ Car. It was there Zinardi enjoyed instant success and became one of the most popular drivers in America. In 2001 while exiting the pit row at the Lausitzring in Germany, he lost control of his car and slid into the path of an oncoming racer. As a result of the crash, Zanardi lost both legs and approximately three-quarters of the blood in his body. It was a true miracle he survived.

But for Alex Zanardi, all the success and tragedy he had experienced up to this point was simply creating the platform for what he would do next. As an engineer and mechanic, he would begin working with his prosthetic team to design his own legs. As he was quoted in Will Buxton's excellent book, *My Greatest Defeat: Stories of Hardship and Hope from Motor Racing's Finest Heroes,* "The functionality of a mechanical knee joint on a prosthetic leg and the similarities it had to the mechanism of the suspension of a race car started this new passion for me."

He has since returned to auto racing on a limited basis with a specially designed BMW. But it was handcycling where Zanardi would achieve ultimate success and global attention. He has won the Venice, Rome, and New York City Marathons. In the 2012 Paralympic Games, Zanardi won two gold medals and a silver. But he wasn't finished. In the 2016 Paralympics, Zanardi won two more gold medals as well as another silver. In the World

Championships, Zanardi is an eight-time gold medal winner while adding two additional silvers. And he is still racing cars and handcycles. So let the medal count continue!

Zanardi said, "The path to creating the conditions that enable you to actually sit in a car and deliver should be the most important part. The most desirable aspect of it all is the journey, not simply crossing the line ahead of everybody else. It is the journey that should interest you and make it fascinating for you. It should be the executing the project, rather than cashing in on the result." He later adds, "If I think back, it was such an enjoyable time of my life, preparing for something like this, not knowing that crossing that (finish) line would have also granted me the glory I had, which was a great reward. But I was not expecting that. It was an added value. The real value was all the time I spent in the wooden shed I have in my garden where I keep all my stuff, training on my bicycle, and then whenever I had nothing else to do, lying next to my bicycle, looking at it, and asking myself how I could make it better and how I could couple it more with my residual talent."

Zinardi's life is a reminder to leaders to focus on the process. Focus on getting better. Focus on getting a great team around you. Focus on your character. Focus on execution. Focus on making marginal gains every day. Focus on complementing your natural talent. But most of all, focus on the journey.

February 23–Changing a Losing Culture into a Winning One

On November 30, 2015, Matt Campbell was named head football coach of the Iowa State Cyclones. Prior to his arrival, Iowa State had won *zero* conference championships since 1912. In fact, they had only been to twelve bowl games in twelve *decades*. However, in the past four seasons, the Cyclones have gone 32–19 including two bowl wins. Coach Campbell has turned this program around.

Some call it a miraculous achievement! In a January 2 ESPN article, he discussed the steps he took to turn Iowa State from a losing culture into a winning one.

Any leader reading this knows that changing a culture is going to be hard work. The leader must have tough skin and be willing to navigate some very difficult waters. Coach Campbell said, "There was a lot of hard road and a lot of tough waters that we had to start back over, clean up and get aligned."

Because it is so difficult, you as a leader must be able to build strong relationships. You must be able to learn from others and develop a network of support. Coach Campbell learned this from his college coach Larry Kehres. As a result, he brought more than a dozen coaches from his previous job at Toledo with him to Iowa State, including both his offensive coordinator Tom Manning and defensive coordinator Jon Heacock. Upon arrival at the school, Coach Campbell knew decisiveness and the courage to make immediate changes would be necessary in establishing a new culture. Former Iowa State wide receiver Allen Lazard, now with the Green Bay Packers, said, "They required new standards, new expectations and held us to a way higher level of accountability that a lot of us—especially me—weren't usually held to."

Tight end Charlie Kolar went on to add, "We don't accept tardiness in this program. In this program, you're on time or you're not practicing that day, doesn't matter who it is." This new level of accountability began showing up on the practice field. Kolar said, "That bleeds over to practice, running the right route, blocking the right gap, making the right tackle."

All of this hard work by Coach Campbell, his staff, and players eventually showed up on the field. With their 2017 upset win over Oklahoma, Coach Campbell said, "Year 1, we had to learn how to believe. In Year 2, we had to learn how to win." He added, "Winning a game like we did against Oklahoma showed us and our kids that, 'Here is what it takes to be successful.'" Did you notice these important steps to turning around a losing culture? First, you had to learn to believe and then you had to learn how to win. Many leaders get the order reversed, and the failure continues despite your best efforts.

Now that the team was beginning to win, Coach Campbell could begin making more strategic changes. During the 2018 season, the team changed its defensive philosophy from a four-man front to three down linemen. Safety Greg Eisworth said, "A lot of it's just been the willingness to really listen and understand the input that players might have. Our coaching staff . . . has had a great deal of success, and they've been doing this for a really long time, so it may be hard to change philosophies or understand what players might be saying."

Finally, changing a losing culture into a winning one is all about the ability to do the fundamentals, the little things, at an elite level. Coach Campbell concluded, "Yes, we've gotten maybe older and our talent has been able to develop, but I think to become the best version of ourselves, the best team that we can become, the difference is in the details. The difference is in our ability to do the little things."

As leaders, take a moment and make an itemized list of all the little things your organization needs to do to be successful. Now take that very same list and give yourself an honest, self-evaluation of how you do those things. After getting the right leader, this is the first step in creating a winning culture.

February 28—Pastor Rusty George

Pastor Rusty George is the lead pastor of Real Life Church in Valencia, California. Operating out of five campuses, he is one of America's greatest pastors. The thing which has always struck me about Pastor Rusty is his calm and soothing demeanor. He just always makes me think God has everything under control, and everything is going to be OK. When I think of all his community endured in 2020 (school shootings, Kobe Bryant's death, COVID, racial riots, and protests), I honestly do not think God could have strategically placed anyone better than Pastor Rusty to walk that community through those difficult and tragic times. He truly pastored the city of Los Angeles through a season unlike any other.

Another reason Pastor Rusty is such a great pastor is he is an incredible Bible teacher. I get a sense many pastors today are confused about their roles. Pastors are not communicators, and they do not give talks. They are messengers of God who give a specific group of people a specific message from God Himself about the specific issues of their life at a specific point in time in human history. A pastor's Sunday sermon should be a message from God Himself, not a TED Talk with a Bible verse tacked on at the end.

March 1—When You're *Not* the Smartest Person in the Room

Lorne Michaels famously said, *"If you're the smartest person in the room, you're in the wrong room."* I am at a fortunate place in my life where I am constantly surrounded by people who are bigger, faster, stronger, smarter, sharper, and godlier than I am. And I have never been happier! I've learned there are people in my circles much more committed to the mission and vision of our organization than I am. In addition, they are more dedicated to perfecting their craft. I've been stretched after watching others have a dedication to detail which far surpasses mine. They simply never seem content with the status quo. It's been humbling but I've seen others put teammates in positions to be far more successful than positions I would have put them in. They also did a far better job equipping them with the tools and resources necessary for those positions.

I like to think I work hard, but I have really been pushed to my limits by others. They were more prepared in every way possible—mentally, physically, and spiritually. This allowed them to take a greater advantage of marginal gains. When it comes to character, I am also currently around people much more generous and humble than I am. Once again, I've never been happier!

This is because I am also keenly aware of how much better I am getting because I am in their presence and gleaning from their wisdom and experience. Are you the smartest person in the rooms you're in? If so, take Michaels' advice and find another room.

March 5—Missing Tom Brady

Tom Brady obviously changed the culture of the Tampa Bay Buccaneers. The great question is exactly how did he do it? On March 5, former NFL head coach Eric Mangini appeared on *The Colin Cowherd Podcast.* As a former New England Patriots assistant coach, he made some very insightful comments on what the Pats missed by not having Tom around last season. First and foremost, Tom Brady is the consummate culture builder. Mangini discussed how Brady "made a lot of things so much better." He made things better both on and off the field.

One of the people Brady helped most from a culture perspective was head coach Bill Belichick. Brady gave Coach Belichick a certain legitimacy with the other players. For instance, if he coached a player of Brady's stature hard, no other player was immune. In addition, if Brady was forced to do something in practice, no other player was afforded the opportunity of saying, "I'm not going to do that." If Brady was doing it, so was everyone else. Mangini said, "And when you don't have Tom Brady going into the locker room and co-signing on things, it's a different dynamic."

But it was what Mangini said next which was so insightful. It had to do with Brady's ability to problem solve. The former coach said, "How many disagreements did he make sure were avoided between the coordinator and a disgruntled receiver or Bill and someone pissed off in the locker room?" Many people did not realize it but Brady was the ultimate peacemaker. Another thing the Patriots missed by not having Brady was his ability to attract other quality free agents. Real recognizes real and like attracts like. Other great players want to play with Tom Brady. There was a reason talented athletes like Rob Gronkowski and Antonio Brown signed with the Buccaneers. They wanted to play with Brady.

But if you play with Brady, you must know it is not always going to be easy. No one has higher standards. Brady was New England's hardest working and most demanding player. These high standards and demand for excellence is what made him such a great player. But just like his willingness to submit to hard coaching, how can you not work hard when the greatest player of all-time is working the hardest of all. But what did the Patriots miss the most by not having Tom Brady on the team?

Not to oversimplify things, but the team missed the play-offs. Brady's new team won the Super Bowl.

March 13—Heath Miller

It's been said no one is irreplaceable. The older I get, the more I realize this may not always be the case. One of my favorite leaders is Pittsburgh Steelers head coach Mike Tomlin. Few leaders can communicate complex truths in such a concise fashion as this great communicator. He would agree with me about the irreplaceability of certain people. At the conclusion of this past season, the team's star tight end Heath Miller retired. Coach Tomlin painted a portrait of what every athlete, employee, and man should strive to become. He summed up his thoughts by saying, "You don't replace a Heath Miller. You simply do the best you can to move on."

As leaders, this comment compels us to closely examine Miller and further understand why he had such an impact on Coach Tomlin. To do so, let's look at his comments leading up to his final statement. Irreplaceable players continually get better. They constantly evolve and improve. This was true of Miller's career. Coach Tomlin commented on having a front-row seat to this player's growth.

Not only did Miller grow on the field, he grew off of it as well as a husband, father, and man. Coach Tomlin said, "To watch him in every way. To watch him raise his sons. To watch his sons get old enough to come to work with him on a Saturday morning." Miller truly epitomized the statement that football is what he did; it was not who he was.

To be irreplaceable, you cannot be high maintenance. Your life must be marked by a lack of drama. Professionalism is your brand. Coach Tomlin pointed it out best by saying, "He's not low maintenance. He's been no maintenance." After reading that quote, all leaders must do some self-examination and see if the same thing could be said about them.

Miller always put the Pittsburgh Steelers organization ahead of his own personal interests in every area of his professional life. With Miller, all decisions were made through the lens of what was best for the team. Coach Tomlin added, "I don't know if there's been a guy like him I've been around from an unselfishness standpoint." He was a true teammate.

Heath Miller played eleven seasons for the Pittsburgh Steelers. He caught 592 passes for 6,569 yards and 45 touchdowns. From a team standpoint, he was the starting tight end on teams that won two Super Bowl championships. But this is not what Coach Tomlin will remember most about him. He admiringly said, "We all fall short, but I don't know if I've ever seen a regrettable moment in him." Coach Tomlin then gave Miller the greatest compliment one grown man can ever give another. He summed up with feelings with "He's the type of person I want my boys to be." As I stated, there's no greater compliment a man can give. These are the reasons Coach Mike Tomlin stated you could not replace Heath Miller. I agree with him.

I also wonder if I'm irreplaceable. There's one way to find out. Would the people I lead and those I report to say the things about me as Coach Tomlin did about Miller if I were gone?

March 21–Dr. Benny Tate

I have heard countless speeches on the subject of leadership. During March's Timothy Barnabas Conference, I heard Dr. Benny Tate, senior pastor for the past thirty-one years of Rock Springs Church in Milner, Georgia, deliver the finest leadership message I have ever heard a pastor give. This is not a hyperbolic statement. Pastor Benny taught a message entitled "Things That Leaders Do That Hinder Their Churches." As I was speaking with him afterward, he said, "Brian, do you know how long it took me to write this message? Thirty-one years." I knew exactly what he meant by that statement, and so do many of you. Sometimes it takes a lifetime to be able to deliver the message of a lifetime.

As you will see below, Pastor Benny's content is so rich and pregnant with implications I want to supply you with as many of his thoughts as possible. The following are sixty-nine quotes from his amazing message:

Seven Things Leaders Do That Hinder Their Churches

Introductory Comments
1. "I'm never gotten tired of the message that Jesus changes lives."
2. "Eighty-five percent of the churches in America pre-COVID were plateaued or declining."
3. "Of the 15 percent that were growing, 14 percent was transfer growth . . . The thing about sheep swapping is you get goats in the mix. Only 1 percent were having salvation growth."
4. "The first church after my ministry closed. The second church I left for health reasons—the deacons got sick of me."

A Foggy Vision
1. "If it's misty in the pulpit, it's foggy in the pews."
2. "You cannot delegate the vision of the church to anyone else. God is going to give the vision of that church to the leader."
3. "God's going to give you the vision, but you have the responsibility to make it gettable."
4. "The vision for your ministry will come from the burden God placed on your heart."
5. "Where there is no vision, people perish. Where there is no vision, people look for another parish."
6. "State the vision clearly."
7. "Cast the vision creatively."

8. "Repeat the vision constantly . . . Your people have to hear something seven times before they hear it once."

9. "Celebrate the vision regularly. Celebrate what you want to see more of."

10. "Embrace the vision personally. You don't teach what you don't know. You don't lead where you don't go."

11. "Vision is where you're going. Vision moves to values—why we are going. That moves to vehicle—how do we get there. We take it from me to we. Velocity—that's the speed. The velocity of the leader determines velocity of the organization."

Refusing to Change

1. "Water is timeless. The method of consumption has changed."

2. "The methods are many. Principles are few. Methods are always changing. Principles never do."

3. "Christianity is all about change."

4. "Life is going to end with a change."

5. "There's no growth without change. There's no change without loss. There's no loss without pain."

6. "When you change something and no one gets angry, you haven't changed anything."

7. "If you're leading, you're bleeding."

8. "Yesterday's home run won't win today's game."—Babe Ruth

9. "I used to teach a message entitled 'Ten Ways to Raise a Spiritually Healthy Child.' And then I had a child."

10. "We're the lid when we refuse to change."

11. "If someone walks over the threshold of our church and they walk back in time, we're in trouble."

12. "A church will quit growing when a pastor refuses to push through the pain."

Trying to Do It All
1. "My responsibility is to discover leaders, develop leaders, and deploy leaders."
2. "When you add followers, you add. When you add leaders, you multiply."
3. "Great preachers don't build great churches. Great churches build great preachers."

We Don't Delegate Because:
1. "A fear of losing authority."
2. "A fear of the work being done poorly."
3. "A fear of the work being done better."
4. "An unwillingness to take the time."
5. "A fear of depending on others ... A growing church has a staff member for every seventy-one people. A church that is not growing has a staff member every fifty people."

Not Understanding the Importance of Those Closest to You
1. "Most leaders in America have a Judas close enough to them to kiss them."—T.D. Jakes
2. "Be slow and prayerful before selecting a team member."
3. "Hire for where you want to go."
4. "Hire people different from you."
5. "If you build a good team, it will have people different from you."

When the Leader Quits Growing Personally
1. "The organization doesn't grow around the leader. The organization grows under the leader."
2. "A lot of men say they have thirty years of experience. Many of them have one year of experience they've repeated thirty times."

3. "God has not called everyone to pastor a mega church. Jesus had 120 when He left. God has called us to be faithful and our churches to be healthy."

Four Dimensions You Need to Lead
1. "Inward Leadership—The toughest person to lead is yourself."
2. "Lateral Leadership—If you're going to lead people laterally, you are going to lead them by serving them."
3. "Upward Leadership—It's leading people when you are under their authority. You're at a dangerous place in your ministry when no one can tell you 'No.'"
4. "Downward Leadership—The Bible talks the least about this and more about the other three."

When the Leader Gets Priorities out of Order
1. "Number one is God."
2. "Number two is your family. Your number one ministry is your family . . . Nobody at home should ever feel like they are competing with somebody at the church. Fight for your families . . . Every day you are absent from your family is gone forever . . . If you can be a good Christian at home, you can be a good Christian anywhere."

When You Doubt What God Can Do Through You
1. "Don't ever doubt what God can do through you."
2. "Death and life are in the power of the tongue."
3. "The place my mother went to end her life, she found her life."
4. "You may not believe what Benny preaches. But Benny believes what Benny preaches."
5. "God is not looking for ability. He's looking for availability."
6. "Your best days are not behind you. Your best days are ahead of you."

7. "It's not time to retire; it's time to refire. The best days are ahead."

Three Things Pastors Should Do for One Another
1. "We need to let others know we're proud of them. It's wrong to have pride in me. It's not wrong for me to be proud of you. And if I'm proud of you and you're proud of me, maybe we wouldn't struggle with pride so much."
2. "Who are you promoting other than you?"
3. "Who are you praying for?"

March 30–The Inner Circle

These are serious times, and we need serious Christian leaders. As a result of dealing with pastors and church leadership teams on a daily basis, I have seen the best and worst of leadership. I have also noticed another trend over the last fifty years. The focus on the first twenty-five years of that time was on *content*—what you say, specifically preaching and teaching Sunday school. The last twenty-five years has been on *creativity*—what you do to find the "Wow Factor." Because of what has happened in our society, the next season of ministry will be focused on *character*—who you are and whether you are the type of person God *can* and *will* use to bring Him glory?

John Maxwell's Law of the Inner Circle teaches that those closest to the leader will determine the leader's success. I could not agree more. Pastors need to pray and ask for divine wisdom when determining who their primary influencers are. The following are the qualities pastors (and all other leaders for that matter) should be looking for in their inner circle:

Members of your inner circle should be first and foremost fiercely loyal. Being loyal does not make you a leader. However, being disloyal disqualifies you as a leader. It is important to add that an inner-circle member must not only be loyal to the leader, but equally important is their loyalty to the mission and vision of the church or organization. In addition, the primary responsibility of a pastor's inner circle is they can hear from God. Their life must be marked by holiness and brokenness before Christ. In short, they are godly people, and it is obvious to everyone that those closest to you are also close to God.

Coupled with this a need to have a biblical worldview. With the complex social issues pastors must deal with today, your inner circle must be able to process all decisions through a biblical lens. Their lives are submitted, popular or unpopular, to what is written in The Book. By the way, the decision for how you handle many issues is already predetermined by Scripture. An additional quality needed in inner-circle members is generosity. Someone who doesn't tithe should never be a part of a pastor's inner circle. It is a clear sign they want influence without the investment. They want a free ride of influence with no cost or responsibility. Also, where you treasure is, there your heart is also. The sad fact is, if they are not tithing, they are not with you.

Generosity is ultimately a matter of trust; do they trust God with what the world trusts most in—money and possessions. Not just with God, but all relationships are built on a foundation of trust. Trustworthy people do what they say they're going to do. Deadlines are met. Promises are kept. Also, they tell the truth. Because the inner-circle is often speaking on behalf of pastors, the church staff, other key leaders, and congregation must be able to trust and have full confidence in them. When people talk to them, they are in essence talking to the pastor.

Some more qualities you should look for in your inner circle:

Members of your inner-circle must evaluate all successes and failures through the grid of your church or organization's mission statement. This removes personal agendas, misevaluations, and the protection of someone's turf. It also elevates organizational effectiveness over personal preferences or relationships. The members of your inner circle must also be your organization's hardest workers. They should arrive first and leave last. Their work ethic will be the standard for your staff and leaders. Your inner circle should always smell like sweat.

The members of a pastor's inner circle must be people of impeccable character. Their lives must be set apart. Sadly, many spiritual leaders I encounter are no longer living lives, which are a reflection of holiness. A pastor's inner circle should never consist of people who cuss, get drunk, cohabitate, smoke weed, or have sex outside the confines of marriage. Leaders always raise the bar. It's time to raise it in the area of personal behavior. Finally, your inner circle must have permission to tell you, "No." You are at a dangerous place in leadership if no one can tell you, "No."

Did you notice I did not list talent? God does not always bless talent, especially if a person's life is marked by sin and foolish living. However, God will always bless those fully devoted to Him.

April 7–The Difference Between Success and Failure

Don't you just grow tired of people who always have an excuse for their failures or blame someone else for their lot in life? Even the most compassionate leaders have a breaking point. So, to help people stop making excuses, the following facts are about people who experience success:

They don't take shortcuts. Successful people know a shortcut today is the fastest way to failure tomorrow. The difference between success and failure is very small. Therefore, the little things matter a great deal. Successful people are willing to pay a greater price than those who aren't. A stark reality is everyone has opportunity to succeed or fail. Some choose to not pay the price or take advantage of their opportunity. Those who do have positioned themselves for success in life.

Your public success is determined by the price you are willing to pay in private. Everyone has to make and remake the decision every day to put in the work and not cut corners. You should never make excuses for failure. Accept responsibility.

April 17—Ten Things I Learned after I Knew It All

I work in an industry where it has been traditionally considered your sweet spot is between the ages of forty-five and fifty-five. There are exceptions to the rule, but in my over twenty years of experience, this has proven to be the case. During this ten-year window, you have the credibility which comes from experience and have some wins under your belt. But you have also made some mistakes and have battle scars to prove it. It is during these years you potentially develop the wonderful combination of experience, relatability, and relevancy. I am now leaving this window. I was thirty-six years old when I joined the company. It is amazing how quickly time has passed.

Sadly, I must now be self-aware enough to know that Father Time is right behind me, chasing me down with each decision I make, and constantly reminding me I run the risk of quickly becoming irrelevant. Few people understand how incredibly hard I work on staying up-to-date and relevant. The following are just some of the things I do:

- Read books every day;

- Write every day;
- Listen to the market's response to my ideas and insights and respond accordingly;
- Hang around younger leaders;
- Work on my health so my mind stays as active as possible;
- Ask lots of questions; and
- Learn something new every day.

It is this last one I want to discuss more in depth. From ages of forty-five to fifty-five, you should become an expert in your craft. You should have put your 10,000 hours by then. You have likely accomplished a great deal but also experienced a number of defeats. As a result, you should also know what *not* to do. You may have seen it all, done it all, learned it all, and even lived to tell about it. But, as someone leaving the forty-five to fifty-five window, I can tell you with great authority that it is what you learned *after* you know it all that counts.

The following are ten things I learned after I knew it all:

1. I learned to focus on God and family first. This sounds like a cliché, but applying this lesson has been a lifelong process. When you stack up all your accomplishments, you quickly come to the realization that the only the thing that really matters is what God and your family think of you.

2. I learned that choosing to invest in the next generation is your greatest return. Thank you to John Maxwell for this lesson. The ones you invest in will be those who keep your ideas, systems, and legacies alive long after you are gone. If you do not invest your wisdom, knowledge, insight, and experiences into someone else, what is inside you dies when you are gone.

3. I learned to become a better listener. Honestly, I am still working on this. My enthusiasm for an idea or rush to

judgment proved disrespectful and capped my level of influence for many years. It is remarkable how much goodwill and influence you gain when you simply just listen to someone's full answer.

4. I learned to be humble or be humbled. Proverbs 16:18 famously tells us, "Pride goes before destruction and a haughty spirit before a fall." The earlier you learn this the better. Stay humble. Stay grateful. Be thankful. If not, life does the work of instilling humility for you.

5. I learned the importance of embracing technology. I am still working on this one as well. We all had to learn Zoom in 2020, but I want to master it. I'm also looking at using Prezi rather than PowerPoint. I am just trying to change and stay relevant.

6. I learned to ask about my blind spots. Jeff Henderson often asks the people in his life, "What's it like being on the other side of me?" I recently asked my team a version of this same question. This takes courage. You had better be ready for the responses and humble enough to listen—and change if necessary.

7. I learned to always be reading books. Stay curious. Always be asking questions. Additional wisdom and knowledge are available just a few clicks away and for literally pennies on the dollar.

8. I learned to do what my daughter wants to do. When it comes to spending time together, it's all about her. As your children leave home and develop their own lives, you really miss them. I have found if I want to spend time with my daughter, it will be on her schedule and agenda. And I'm OK with that. I'm even learning to enjoy overpriced, trendy coffee shops!

9. I have learned the importance of continually producing results. Do your job with excellence! The best way for anyone to stay relevant and respected is to continually

produce results. You can never argue with the bottom line. Your personal health is a major contributor to this. Also, it is important to stop telling war stories and successes from twenty years ago. First, no one cares. Second, it gives the impression your best days are behind you and makes you look pitiful and foolish. It is what you are doing today and where you are going tomorrow that counts.

10. I learned the importance of simply being nice. If not, you will be labeled as "the grumpy old man who is out of touch, clinging to the past, and unable to change." Also, most major decisions are made about you when you're not in the room. Therefore, you want people saying nice things about you when you are not there. Once again, be nice! Flowers grow from the rain, not the thunder.

11. And, the bonus nugget: Most importantly, I learned how much more there was to learn after I knew it all.

April 26—Nick Saban's Two Most Important Words About Creating Value for Yourself

"People are looking for reasons not to pick you. They're looking for reasons not to hire you. So don't give anyone a reason to say, 'BUT.' That's the only way you can create value for yourself." —Alabama Crimson Tide Head Coach Nick Saban

As previously mentioned, most decisions made about your career are made when you are not in the room. Think about it. You were not there when someone in the admissions office approved your application to college. You were not in the room when it was decided you would be promoted, given a salary increase, or retained during a time of layoffs and cutbacks. Therefore, since you are not in these rooms, you will need advocates in the room who will represent you well and say nice things about you to others.

Coach Saban needs no introduction to anyone who is interested in leadership. With the NFL Draft about to take place, he took the time to give an interview on how leaders can create value for themselves. He knows his players are being talked about in NFL circles they are not in and teaches them how they can maximize their value. Coach Saban puts players (and leaders for that matter) into one of two categories: "And People" or "But People." Allow him to explain. Coach Saban said, "I tell our players all the time the two most compelling words in the Draft report is 'and' and 'but.'"

He explains an "and" person does this, this, and this well—*and*. The coach then gave some examples, "*And* he's a good person. He was a leader on the team. He graduated from school. The coaches loved him."

The contrast, though, is the person who does this, this, and this well—*but*. *But* he had a positive drug test. He had a domestic violence incident with his girlfriend. He got in a fight in the bar when he was a freshman. The strength coach said he wouldn't piss on him if he was on fire."

Then he asks his players and those listening the obvious question, "Who do you want on your team—*And* or *But*?" Coach Saban then evaluated reality, "You don't realize as soon as you apply for a job, as soon as you put your name in for the Draft, people are looking for reasons not to pick you. They're looking for reasons not to hire you. So don't give anyone a reason to say, '*but.*' That's the only way you can create value for yourself." He then summarized his thoughts prior to the NFL Draft by asking, "How do I create value for myself? I might have to edit my behavior a little bit."

So the question is obvious—Are you an "*And* leader" or a "*But* leader"? If you are a "*But* leader," what edits are you willing to make in your leadership to reverse this perception of yourself?

Interestingly, the pre-draft coverage centered on Green Bay Packers superstar quarterback Aaron Rodgers and his potential desire to be traded. My initial leadership thought is you can't leap-frog leaders. Prior to Green Bay's moving up into the first round of the 2020 Draft to select quarterback Jordan Love, Rodgers should have at least been consulted. Whether he agreed with the organization's decision or not, as the face of the franchise, he should not have found out the team's decision by watching the Draft like the normal rank and file. Another lesson we learn from this situation is the top performers in your organization should be supported in every manner possible—financially, emotionally, supporting personnel, and resources. When organizations minimize top performers or take them for granted, institutional dysfunction ensues. ESPN's Booger McFarland summed it up by saying, "There is no one to blame but the GM at Green Bay." Louis Riddick added, "If you don't communicate with your star quarterback who has personality issues, that's on you."

Now, my thoughts on the first fifteen picks of the first round. These insights flow from the comments made by ESPN's broadcast team which I will include. Leaders must minimize what their teams do not do well. As expected, the Jacksonville Jaguars selected Clemson Tigers quarterback Trevor Lawrence with the first pick. McFarland noted, "They are going to have to protect him, then minimize what he doesn't do well."

With the second pick, the New York Jets selected BYU quarterback Zach Wilson. From Wilson, we learn that great leaders continually improved. Draft expert Mel Kiper said of him, "The improvement he showed this year from 2019 and 2018 was incredible . . . He went from 62 percent completion in 2019 to 73.5 this year. He went from eleven touchdown passes to thirty."

How much are great leaders worth? The San Francisco 49ers would tell you to pay whatever price is needed to get the right leader for your team. They traded three first-round picks and a 2022 third-round pick for the privilege of selecting North Dakota State quarterback Trey Lance. Even the best leaders need support. This was evident when the Atlanta Falcons selected Florida Gators tight end Kyle Pitts with the fourth selection. Referencing the Aaron Rodgers situation in Green Bay, Kiper said of the generational talent, "One (Green Bay Packers) didn't support the quarterback. One organization did in the selection of Kyle Pitts."

You cannot undersell the value of chemistry when it comes to leadership. Leaders must feel comfortable with the people they surround themselves with. We were reminded of this principle when the Cincinnati Bengals selected LSU Tigers wide receiver Ja'Marr Chase with the fifth pick. In 2020, newly-selected franchise quarterback Joe Burrow was sacked thirty-two times in just ten games. In addition, he suffered a season-ending knee injury. Burrow needed to be protection, and Oregon Ducks tackle Penei Sewell seemed like the perfect fit. However, they went with Burrow's former teammate, wide receiver Chase, who caught twenty touchdown passes from Burrow on the team's 2019 national championship club. Chemistry matters.

With the next selection, the Miami Dolphins chose the explosive wide receiver from Alabama Jaylen Waddle. What leaders need to understand about this pick is the importance of adding as many difference-makers to your team as possible. Difference-makers are those individuals whose mere presence and skill set can change the fortunes of your team. These type of people are rare and, therefore, hard to find. While at Alabama, Waddle scored seventeen touchdowns averaging 44.5 yards. He is a home-run hitter. Riddick said, "He is an angle destroyer. He is going to get the ball and run away from everyone else."

With the seventh pick, the Detroit Lions selected Sewell. Several scouts told McFarland, "If you could count on one guy to be a Hall of Famer, it would be Penei Sewell." The challenge for Sewell and all leaders is knowing what your full potential is and then having a plan to develop your talent and achieve it. Let's hope the Detroit Lions have one for this potentially generational talent.

Smart teams are commit to a process and stick to it. The Carolina Panthers utilized every pick in the 2020 Draft on defensive players. They continued this trend by selecting South Carolina cornerback Jaycee Horn. Mel Kiper noted, "They are committed to the defense." Yes, they are. Is your organization as equally committed to its process?

The first mild surprise in the Draft occurred with the Denver Broncos' selection of cornerback Patrick Surtain II with the ninth overall pick. What is noticeable about Surtain is his mastery of the basics of his position. McFarland said, "He's been coached by Nick Saban who coaches the DBs. He's a technically, fundamentally-sound corner." All great leaders know the little everyday things are as important as big flashy things. How you and your team do anything is how you do everything.

Great leaders produce results. The Philadelphia Eagles moved up from the twelfth position in the first round to the tenth slot taking the Cowboys' pick and selected Alabama wide receiver and Heisman Trophy winner DeVonta Smith. The Cowboys also received a third-round pick in the deal. Riddick said of Smith, "They need someone who has produced at a high level in college . . . He is just a big play waiting to happen . . . As a group, the Philadelphia Eagles had the third-lowest receiving yards in the league last year." Something else you can add is: successful leaders solve problems.

In the 2017 NFL Draft, Chicago Bears general manager Ryan Pace selected North Carolina quarterback Mitch Trubisky with the second pick. Pace selected Trubisky over probable Hall of Famers Patrick Mahomes and Deshaun Watson who went eight and ten picks later, respectively. In this year's Draft, the team got aggressive and moved up from the twentieth spot to number 11 and selected their quarterback of the future, Ohio State's Justin Fields. Here's the leadership lesson—we all need second chances, and everyone loves a redemption story. Maybe the selection of Fields will prove to be a chance at redemption for Ryan Pace.

With great leaders comes an assumption of problem solving. You feel this when a leader walks into the room during a strategy or planning meeting. Everyone breathes a sigh of relief because (fill in the name) has arrived. People then ask, "Hey, we're facing a problem here. What do you think?" Or, when the leader walks in the room, it is like a balloon deflating. Creativity shuts down. Collaboration shuts down. The leader creates more problems. The phrase you hear is, "Things were going fine until (fill in the name) got here."

Leadership is about problem-solving.

With the twelfth pick of the Draft, the Dallas Cowboys solved a lot of problems with the selection of Penn State linebacker Micah Parsons. Last year, the Cowboys gave up 473 points (the most in franchise history), 158.8 rush yard per game (31st in the NFL), and 5.0 yards per rush (thirtieth in the NFL). I think the right leader just walked in the door.

Experienced leaders know the value that luck plays into a team's success. Sometimes the right things need to fall into place for you. I once heard a pastor say, "Luck is when God chooses to remain anonymous." Well, God must have remained anonymous when it came to the San Diego Chargers selection of Northwestern tackle Rashawn Slater with the thirteenth pick. In the 2020 Draft, the Chargers selected franchise quarterback and surefire superstar Justin Herbert. The team's top priority this year was to protect their investment, and Slater fell right to them. Never discount the value of luck!

Speaking of protecting your investment, the Jets traded up to the fourteenth position to select USC tackle Alijah Verra-Tucker after drafting quarterback Zach Wilson with the second pick. Something else we learn from Verra-Tucker is smart leaders do not make unnecessary mistakes. Kiper said, "He had only two holding penalties in 849 snaps and allowed only two sacks."

Maybe the most important lesson for all young leaders happened with the fifteenth selection. Alabama quarterback Mac Jones fell to the New England Patriots. The dynasty continues!

Here's the lesson—when you are a young leader, don't look for great money. Look for great cultures and great management. Money can be fleeting. But if you are part of a great culture, your sustainability and opportunity for personal and economic growth is much greater.

I want to conclude my review of the 2021 NFL Draft with the college recruiting statistics from the first round.

- Seven of the thirty-two selections were five-star prospects coming out of high school;
- Ten were four-star prospects;
- Seven of the top twelve selections were ranked in the Top 100 in their recruiting class;
- Alabama had six first-round selections—more than the Pac 12 and Big 12 combined. They also tied the ACC; and

- The SEC, as a conference, led the way with twelve of the thirty-two first round picks (37.5%).

May 2-Thirteen Characteristics of a Great Sermon

Nothing changes a human heart like the preaching of the Word of God. In addition, nothing grows a church faster than better preaching. Over 100 years ago, the legendary Charles Haddon Spurgeon felt a deep desire to impress on others the importance of preaching and the components of a great sermon. In his treatise *Lectures to My Students,* he wrote these convicting words:

> *Sermons should have real teaching in them, and their doctrine should be solid, substantial, and abundant. We do not enter the pulpit to talk for talk's sake; we have instructions to convey important to the last degree, and we cannot afford to utter petty nothings. Our range of subjects is all but boundless and we cannot, therefore, be excused if our discourses are threadbare and devoid of substance. If we speak as ambassadors for God, we need never complain of want of matter, for our message is full to overflowing. The entire gospel must be presented from the pulpit; the whole faith once delivered to the saints must be proclaimed by us. The truth as it is in Jesus must be instructively declared so that the people may not merely hear, but know, the joyful sound . . . Nothing can compensate for the absence of teaching.*

As you read them, it feels they are more relevant today than ever before. After reading his thoughts, the following are "Thirteen Characteristics of a Great Sermon":

1. A Great Sermon Has Real Teaching—"Sermons should have real teaching in them"

2. A Great Sermon Has Solid Doctrine—"and their doctrine should be solid." It is biblically accurate.

3. A Great Sermon Has Content with Great Worth and Value—"substantial." It has meaning.

4. A Great Sermon Has Plentiful Content—"abundant." Get ready to take a lot of notes!

5. A Great Sermon Is Not a "Talk"—"We do not enter the pulpit to talk for talk's sake." Preachers are not communicators. See more on Point 9.

6. A Great Sermon Is Important and Relevant—"We have instructions to convey important to the last degree."

7. A Great Sermon Is Not Shallow—"We cannot afford to utter petty nothings."

8. A Great Sermon Is Delivered by an Equipped Pastor Possessing a Great Breadth and Depth of Biblical Knowledge—"Our range of subjects is all but boundless and we cannot, therefore, be excused if our discourses are threadbare and devoid of substance."

9. A Great Sermon Is in Actuality a Message from God—Pastors are not communicators and do not give talks. They deliver a message on behalf of God for His people at a specific moment and time in human history. Spurgeon wrote, "If we speak as ambassadors for God"

10. Pastors Who Preach Great Sermons Never Lack for Content—"We need never complain of want of matter, for our message is full to overflowing." If you preach verse-by-verse through entire books of the Bible, you will *never* run out of content.

11. A Great Sermon Presents the Entire Gospel—"The entire gospel must be presented from the pulpit; the whole faith once delivered to the saints must be proclaimed by us."

12. A Great Sermon Instructively Declares Jesus—"The truth as it is in Jesus must be instructively declared so that the people may not merely hear, but know, the joyful sound."

13. Nothing Can Compensate for a Great Sermon—"Nothing can compensate for the absence of teaching."

So the questions begs, pastors, would Spurgeon say you are delivering great sermons on a weekly basis?

May 10–Signs Pastors Do Not Respect Their Elder Board

I work with a lot of churches. It is always fascinating to me how the pastors and staff view their elders (or lay leadership) and how they are subsequently utilized. Some pastors and church staff deeply respect and honor the office of elder and the individuals who hold it. They are true partners in ministry and valued partners and spiritual guides. Others, however, take a different route. They have little to no respect for their elders. I can always tell when this is the case. The following are the warning signs which indicate to me when a lack of respect exists.

The church staff does not value or respect their leaders. You see, the leader sets the tone for the entire organization. In a church's case, this will be the senior pastor. If the senior pastor does not respect the elder board or value their input, this will filter to the staff who will do likewise. Another tell-tell sign is when the elders are not included before critical church decisions are made. Nothing shows disrespect more for a leader than finding out critical information at the same time as the rank and file. When the pastor and staff choose to leapfrog these leaders, it is an indication of a lack of respect.

Meetings are another indicator. Does the pastor meet with his elder board often? If not, it is a sign he sees no value in regularly getting together. When done properly, an elder meeting should be highly encouraging and of great strategic value to the pastor.

If there is no encouragement or strategic value taking place, then there will be no regular meetings as well.

The pastors and staff patronize them. Appointments are made for political reasons. They give certain people positional leadership to make them feel like insiders but never grant them true influence. They tell them what they need to tell them and what they want to hear to get them to do what they want them to do.

One of the worst signs of disrespect is when pastors never invest in the elder boards from a leadership perspective. Personal growth is simply not a priority. How are they supposed to get better unless you train and equip them? Another is when the pastors and staff push back when excellence is demanded of them by the elders. The elders are viewed nuisances and hindrances to their personal comfort or ruts.

Subsequently, the pastors and staff then neutralize their influence and ignore their ministry involvement. The phrase you hear is, "We've got this," or the staff feels they bring no value so why give them the time of day? This behind-the-scenes mentality then filters into the public arena and weekend services. The elders have no role in public ministry. They are not tasked with in-service praying for people, decision counseling, new member training, or any public platform presence. In this environment, the elders are certainly not included in personnel decisions or the details of the church's finances.

The elders are never referred to by the pastor or staff. They are simply names on a page and only engaged when the pastor or staff need a backstop for unpopular decisions. One area of concern which is often not discussed is the pastor's personal time. If the pastor does not spend individual time with his elders away from the office, if he does see them as friends in the journey, there will certainly be a lack of respect.

If this describes you or your staff, be reminded of these verses:

- "Is anyone among you sick? Let him call for the elders of the church, and let them pray over him, anointing him with oil in the name of the Lord." —James 5:14 (ESV)
- "If anyone is above reproach, the husband of one wife, and his children are believers and not open to the charge of debauchery or insubordination. For an overseer, as God's steward, must be above reproach. He must not be arrogant or quick-tempered or a drunkard or violent or greedy for gain, but hospitable, a lover of good, self-controlled, upright, holy, and disciplined. He must hold firm to the trustworthy word as taught, so that he may be able to give instruction in sound doctrine and also to rebuke those who contradict it." —Titus 1:6–9 (ESV)
- "Pay careful attention to yourselves and to all the flock, in which the Holy Spirit has made you overseers, to care for the church of God, which he obtained with his own blood." —Acts 20:28 (ESV)

I want to end this chapter with a warning for elders. You will give an account before God of how you stewarded your role as an elder. Make sure you steward it well. One way to ensure this is to wholeheartedly serve the staff and church (Mark 10:45) and not become intoxicated by power and controlling your pastor and staff. Elders, pastors, and church staff together is a sacred partnership after all.

May 13–Dabo Swinney

Regardless of what industry you are in, there a few people who are better culture builders than Clemson Tigers head football coach

Dabo Swinney. On Wednesday, May 12, Coach Swinney appeared as a guest on *The Colin Cowherd Podcast*. The topics they covered ranged from his upbringing to his recruiting philosophy of Trevor Lawrence. But the best part of the conversation centered on the culture he has built at Clemson. Coach Swinney often states the Clemson program exists to serve the players' hearts, not their talent. It is a "developmental, relationship-driven program." As he pointed out in the interview, "1.7% of college players play in the NFL and it's a shame we make it all about that."

So what does this look like from a practical standpoint. It begins in the recruiting process. Coach Swinney and his staff do not avoid red flags potential recruits may have. He leads with his faith and prioritizes education and a sense of family. Education is priority with Coach Swinney because he said, "I've had a lot of great experiences but walking across that stage at Alabama and getting my degree made me different from everyone else in my family, and it gave me opportunities my mom and dad didn't get in life." Players who do not attend class do not play in the games. As a result, the Tigers have had a 98 percent graduation rate since Coach Swinney took over the program.

Coach Swinney and the Clemson Tigers also strive for consistency. Consistency is a sign of greatness because it shows you can excel for an extended period of time. Part of having consistent success is the ability to always be looking ahead and be forward-thinking. Coach Swinney compares it to mountain climbing: "It's like climbing a mountain every year. You don't get to stay on the mountain. Every year we're back at the bottom."

The following are some of his additional thoughts on never being complacent with success:

- "I'm always building . . . The life cycle of anything—The birth, you've got growth. You've got plateau. You got decline. You got death. The key is to never plateau."
- "You've always got to recommit, refocus, restart, recharge, reinvest, reinstall."
- "Greatness is always under construction."

Because the program is so heavily focused on character, academics, family, faith, and looking ahead, it is an honor to receive a scholarship offer from Clemson. They consistently rank in the bottom-five for number of offers made to potential recruits. But you can't argue with the team's culture or success.

Coach Swinney concluded the interview by saying, "Nine out of the last ten years (we've) been in the Top 10 academically . . . The last ten years we've been second in the country in wins, second in draft picks, since I've been a head coach. We've built a model of consistency and we've done it our way." It's a way other programs need to model.

May 15—Five Things We Must Communicate for a Sermon or Speech to Be Effective

The ability to communicate is an essential quality to develop in every leader's life. This is because at some point, every leader must stand before their team of people and say, "Follow me!" Your ability to communicate, as well as the level of trust you have built up and your track record of success, will largely determine the level of their response. The Bible is the greatest leadership book ever written. It is my primary go-to resource when I want to improve my ability to positively influence people.

In 2 Timothy 4:1–2, the apostle Paul, just prior to his death, writes to his protégé and son in the faith, Timothy, the following words:

"I charge you in the presence of God and of Jesus Christ, who is to judge the living and the dead, and by his appearing and his Kingdom: preach the Word; be ready in season and out of season; reprove, rebuke, and exhort, with complete patience and teaching."(ESV) Paul was uniquely qualified to tell us how to preach. His words echo to us some 2,000 years later. When it comes time for us to give an effective speech or sermon, Paul gives us the following five things we must communicate:

Reprove

For a speech or sermon to be effective, it must begin by exposing an error or inefficiency in our lives or organizations. There must be a problem to solve. Pastors must address the issue that is keeping us from reaching our God-given potential. For the Christian or church attender listening to their pastor, this would be sin—the thing which separates us from God.

Rebuke

Now that the sin issue has been identified and exposed, you must address the issue. You must encourage those listening to change, to grow, and to repent. Depending on your audience and their level of understanding of the issue, you will possibly need to even scold, chide, or correct.

Exhort

The "hard" message has now been delivered. It is both appropriate and logical to then offer hope and encouragement. Within the context of your personality, the pastor or speaker must now lovingly urge the audience to move toward a better way of life. Exhortation involves some combination or encouragement, support, comfort, and aid in taking their next steps.

Complete Patience

Let's remember who is giving the instruction here. To be able to deliver his message, the apostle Paul said in 2 Corinthians 11:24–28 (ESV):

> *Five times I received at the hands of the Jews the forty lashes less one. Three times I was beaten with rods. Once I was stoned. Three times I was shipwrecked; a night and a day I was adrift at sea; on frequent journeys, in danger from rivers, danger from robbers, danger from my own people, danger from Gentiles, danger in the city, danger in the wilderness, danger at sea, danger from false brothers; in toil and hardship, through many a sleepless night, in hunger and thirst, often without food, in cold and exposure. And, apart from other things, there is the daily pressure on me of my anxiety for all the churches.*

I doubt you would face what Paul did, but depending on your message, your audience may or may not be receptive. In today's culture, you may even receive significant backlash or hostility for your words. In particular, pastors must be willing to move forward despite opposition and be longsuffering with their audience and the process.

Teaching

This is where mistakes are often made. The message given by pastors and presenters must contain and conclude with pragmatic, intellectual instruction as to the next steps in their audience's lives. Here is a phrase I recommend which has worked well, "Here's what I want you to do . . ."

Let's do a quick recap:

1. Reprove—Expose error in the listeners' lives.
2. Rebuke—Speak out against it.
3. Exhort—Urge and encourage change.
4. Complete Patience—Expect opposition but move forward anyway.
5. Teaching—Give emotional and intellectual instruction.

Do these five things to position yourself for a great speech or sermon.

May 17–Six Things All Leaders Must Know About Dealing with Selfish Team Members

Each Monday morning, I have the privilege of being part of a Zoom Bible study for baseball scouts and coaches. It is arguable my favorite forty-five minutes of the week. Today's lesson centered on what it meant to be a wholehearted follower of Jesus Christ.

Former manager of the Colorado Rockies and Pittsburgh Pirates Clint Hurdle was asked if he ever managed any players who were all about themselves. Coach Hurdle enthusiastically responded with a profile of what a selfish team member looks like. First, selfish team members are all-in on the team's goals until it costs them something personally. When personal sacrifice is then required for the overall good of the team, selfish players self-identify themselves by often being unwilling to pay that price. One of the ways you can recognize selfish players is they become what Coach Hurdle calls "I's." The I's players say things like, "I want to pitch on opening day. I want to pitch when we open a series. I want to pitch during the day." Coach Hurdle was emphatic: you must separate the I's from the other players.

How do you do it? Selfishness demands tough conversations. Coach Hurdle would confront them in the privacy of his office.

He was careful never to do this in public. Part of this discussion would include the impact of this behavior on their teammates. Coach Hurdle would tell them in no uncertain terms, "Your teammates are watching you."

Sometimes however, even coaching and confrontation cannot pull the selfishness out of someone. If this is the case, a post-season evaluation and hard decisions must be made. Part of Coach Hurdle's evaluation process was to line up each player side-by-side in his mind and ask "Is he in?"

Few things are as joyful as leading a team of unselfish individuals. It's what every coach and leader dreams of. Coach Hurdle told those listening, "When you have a large group of men who are in, you'll have the best year ever." Coach Clint Hurdle is a man of great wisdom. The proof is in the pudding. As a major league manager, he won 1,269 games. He truly is an expert on the subject of leadership.

May 18–Twenty-One Things Pastors Did During COVID I Want To Thank Them For

Tomorrow morning, I have been asked to speak to a group of local government officials and pastors. It is a humbling assignment. When I asked what topic I should discuss, the response was "leadership and hope." After much prayer and wrestling through a myriad of options, the following is what I will be sharing with them. I want them to be seen, heard, and valued. Therefore, I will identify the following twenty-one things pastors did During COVID I want to thank them for:

1. I want to thank them for all the extra prayers they prayed;
2. I want to thank them for all the extra phone calls they made to church members to see how they were doing;

3. I want to thank them for all the extra planning meetings they had to attend and lead;
4. I want to thank them for all the extra "suggestions" they received on masks, openings and closings, racial items, and much, much more;
5. I want to thank them for all the extra compassion and grace they then needed to show;
6. I want to thank them for all the extra Sundays they had to preach;
7. I want to thank them for all the extra days and hours they worked;
8. I want to thank them for all the extra care and concern they showed us when we returned to church. This showed up in all the sanitary adjustments they needed to make for the bathrooms, childrens' areas, fumigating between services, signage, and seating strategies;
9. I want to thank them for all the extra visits they made to senior adult homes;
10. I want to thank them for all their extra service to the community;
11. I want to thank them for all the extra equipping they did for their staffs;
12. I want to thank them for all the extra love they showed their families and loved ones. It was their first pandemic too;
13. I want to thank them for all the extra skills they needed to develop, such as preaching to and through a camera, technology, preaching funerals and weddings differently, preaching to people in cars, and learning to be homeschool teachers;
14. I want to thank them for their humility and commitment to personal growth;
15. I want to thank them for preaching the Word to us. We needed a shepherd more than ever;
16. I want to thank them for challenging us;

17. I want to thank them for calling us to commitment despite extraordinarily difficult circumstances;
18. I want to thank them for giving us stability;
19. I want to thank them for giving us next steps in our faith;
20. I want to thank them for giving us hope; and
21. Most of all, I want to thank them for their resilience. I want to thank them for not quitting and continuing to keep coming back week after week. The world is a better place because they showed up for work every day.

I trust my message will honor them and gives them solid leadership principles. I hope it does for you as well.

May 22–Why Great Organizations, Teams, and People Are Destroyed from Within

In 2020, Ethan Sherwood Strauss wrote a revealing book entitled *The Victory Machine: The Making and Unmaking of the Warriors Dynasty*. The Warriors he is referring to are the former three-time NBA champion Golden State Warriors. While every key member of the team, coaching staff, ownership, and executive management are featured, the book places heavy emphasis on stars Steph Curry and Kevin Durant. On the May 19 edition of *The Colin Cowherd Podcast*, Strauss discussed the Warriors and gave his thoughts on why NBA dynasties are so hard to maintain. When you listen to his thoughts, you begin to see why the '90s Chicago Bulls, the Shaq-Kobe Lakers, and the Golden State Warriors did not have success longer than they did. Most great organizations, teams, and people are destroyed from within because of ego. Strauss said, "In football, it is age and injury that unseats the dynasty. In the NBA it's almost always ego."

He went on to discuss how people drift toward being more focused on their personal interests rather than the overall good of the team.

A scarcity mindset can set in. In many professions, you are judged by what you produce. For basketball players and for scorers like Curry, Durant, and shooting guard Klay Thompson, there are only so many shots to go around. Strauss added, "Your statistics come at the expense of one another." He went on to add, "In baseball, if I'm hitting thirty home runs, I'm helping you in the order. I'm helping you; it's protection. It's all for the good. That's not how the NBA is."

Teams can become destroyed from within because so many leaders are unable to give credit away. They do not understand a match loses none of its fire or light when it lights another match. Sadly, the Warriors, as well as many of us, feel differently. Strauss pointed out, "These guys from a very early age have an exquisite understanding that one guy's credit comes at my expense." Finally, being destroyed from within comes down to teammates who are no longer willing to sacrifice for each other. Strauss concluded his thoughts by saying, "The whole endeavor of winning a championship is this act of sacrifice, and it's almost like balancing on a log that's spinning. It can only go for so long until somebody gets mad because the championship is just not satisfying their ego and it's not fulfilling them like the sacrifice requires."

I have been part of some great organizations which were destroyed from within. These organizations were filled with people no longer willing to balance on and spin the log. Much like the Golden State Warriors, it was because of their ego, selfishness, greed, and thirst for glory. In a single word—hubris. There was really no difference between the NBA champions and your typical church staff or business. It was always about "me" more than "we." If you want to have a sustained run of excellence at your organization, my recommendation is to learn from the Golden State Warriors. It is not too late to make the proper course corrections. If not, you will be destroyed from within as well.

May 23–Things That Make Change Worth Doing

No one likes change but a baby, especially me. At the time of this writing, I have been married for thirty years, had the same hairstyle since the early '80s (only thinner), both of our cars have over 230,000 miles, and I have had the same job for nineteen years. But this past week, I took a risk, changed something in my life, and it turned out pretty good. In addition to the items mentioned above, my family has also lived at our current home since 2003. When we moved here, it was a new subdivision. As a result, everything was brand new. The grass was new. The trees and the shrubs were new. The appliances were new. The carpet was new. The paint had that new fresh paint smell. Everything was new.

But an interesting thing happened over the next decade: As the trees grew taller and taller, their growing root system sucked up all the water and coupled with the expansive shade, killed all the grass under them. The barren parts in my yard resulted in letters from our homeowners association. This was extremely frustrating. The trees they planted killed the grass they planted and was now resulting in threatening letters containing terms like "fines" and "lien." I managed this issue for several years with extensive landscaping work but have just grown sick of it. It was time for my beloved trees to come down. I had to deal with the issue. It was time for change. A tree service was employed to give my yard a permanent facelift. I learned many things about the subject of change through this process.

Change is worth doing when it becomes necessary. Typically, I change only when forced to. Maybe you are better at this than I am. But I knew if I didn't make significant steps toward improvements in my yard, the homeowners association would be making recommendations for me. And let's just say their recommendations would be quite costly.

Change comes easier when recommended by a trusted voice. This tree service was recommended by a friend who had this same team take down approximately a dozen trees in his own yard. A reference sale is always the best sale. As I went through this process, change became easier as my confidence in a positive outcome grew. When I reached out to the tree service, they were very timely in their response and coming to our home for estimates. The owner was very professional and made recommendations I did not even think of.

Change was easier because the price was less than I anticipated. The cost is where plans to change usually go to die. Often, the price for change is not worth paying. Even though taking trees down and laying sod is quite expensive, I felt the price quoted was more than fair. This was just another step in my growing confidence in this company. As mentioned earlier, change comes easier when recommended by a trusted voice. Change also comes easier when done in partnership with experts. The individuals taking down the trees were not only experts, they were artists. They were efficient, timely, and masters of their craft.

Finally, change is worth doing when you see the results. Bottom line, my yard has never looked better. When I turn down my street, I am very proud to look at my yard. I will be hiring his team for additional projects this fall. Moving forward, when considering if it is time for a change or not, I will ask the following questions:

1. Is it necessary?
2. Am I getting good recommendations on who to help me?
3. Do I have high confidence in the process after meeting them?
4. Am I willing to pay the price?
5. Are my partners in the process experts?
6. Will I enjoy the results?

If the answer to each of these six questions is "Yes," it is time to change.

This process of change was a great experience for me. Will it make me more open to the idea of change in the future? I don't know. No one likes change but a baby—especially still me.

June 1—The Glue That Holds Teams Together

In Buster Olney's book *The Last Night of the Yankee Dynasty: The Game, the Team, and the Cost of Greatness,* he writes:

> *It was shortly after (manager Joe) Torre had surgery for prostate cancer, in the spring of 1999, that (pitching coach Mel) Stottlemyre told him of his own condition (multiple myeloma—cancer of the bone marrow), which would be monitored for a year before he required more extensive treatment. Darryl Strawberry's cancer was diagnosed five months before Torre's, and less than three years after Torre's brother, Rocco had died; another brother, Frank, had required a heart transplant in the midst of the 1996 World Series.*

Olney continues: *"The fathers of four Yankees veterans passed away during the championship run: Maury Brosius, Chick O'Neal, Ambrosio Sojo, and Bernabe Williams. Real life constantly invaded the Yankees' baseball world,"* And then Olney concludes with this thought: *"and after Mike Stanton left the team, he concluded that the reason this group of teammates had become so close was that they had needed one another so often."*

I have four co-workers who I have spent the majority of the last two decades with. We have gone through a lot together as well. The following is just a small sampling:

- We've been there for each other when we've buried parents, close friends, and in one case, a son.
- Two had daughters whose weddings I attended.
- One of my four friends got married and now has a wonderful family.
- We walked through the 2008 financial crisis and the 2020 pandemic together.
- We've been through the sale of the company on two separate occasions.
- We've watched our children grow up and become successful adults.
- We've all gotten some gray hair together.
- We've put off the aging process as much as we can.
- And I could go on and on.

So what does my band of brothers and the New York Yankees of the 1990s have in common? It goes back to Mike Stanton's words. We've needed each other on countless occasions. The glue no one talks about that truly creates unity and holds teams together is lasting relationships and shared experiences. It's the equity of weathering a series of storms together. It's laughing together on the road so hard your sides hurt, bearing one another's burdens, and celebrating each other's success.

It is highly unlikely teams with high turnover rates will have the time to develop the glue needed to have unity during the most stressful and challenging times. It takes some time and having each other's backs over and over again to build trust and unity. You've got to go through some stuff together and live to tell about it. And you must show each other a lot of grace along the way.

In conclusion, hire good people who are talented. Be willing to then play the long game. Celebrate the good times and build each other up during the bad ones. You'll win some, and you'll lose some.

The Lord giveth and the Lord taketh away. Blessed be the name of the Lord. And if you're lucky, after five-to-ten years, you'll be glad you did because there will be an uncommon glue that holds your whole team, perhaps your whole organization, together.

June 6—Devin Booker Becomes a Superstar

On Thursday, June 3rd, 2021, the Phoenix Suns defeated LeBron James and the Los Angeles Lakers 113–100, allowing the Suns to win their first-round series of the NBA playoffs four-games to two. History will remember many things about this series. First is defending champion James having to experience a first-round exit. Second is the incomparable TNT announcer Charles Barkley referring to often-injured Anthony Davis as "Street Clothes." But most importantly, this series will be remembered as the moment when the Phoenix Suns's Devin Booker officially became a star. If you wish to become the star of your organization, there are several things we can learn from Booker.

First, stars are not always recognizable. Booker was not the first pick of the 2015 NBA Draft. That honor went to Kentucky's Karl Anthony-Towns. In fact, he was not the second (D'Angelo Russell) or third pick (Jahlil Okafor). Moreover, he was not the first, second (Willie Cauley-Stein), or third (Trey Lyles) player drafted from the University of Kentucky. Devin Booker fell to the thirteenth pick of the Draft by the Phoenix Suns. We also learn that becoming a star is not a solo act. You need talent around you. The Suns added future Hall of Fame Chris Paul along with lottery picks Mikal Bridges, Cam Johnson, and Deandre Ayton to assist him.

To become a star you not only need talent around you, you need talented leadership. The Suns general manager James Jones hired the outstanding head coach Monty Williams. Jones was named the league's Executive of the Year. Williams was a Coach of the Year finalist. The acquisition of these individuals aided in not only Booker's personal ascension but the team's as well. The Suns improved from a record of 34–39 (47% winning percentage) in 2020 to 51–21 (71%) this year. It has often been said that big-time players make big-time plays in big-time games. In the closeout game against the Lakers, Booker had twenty-two first-quarter points on eight-of-nine shooting, making all six of his threes. He finished with forty-seven points. Shaquille O'Neal said afterward, "This is what superstars do in closeout games. Give me the damn ball and get out the way."

Devin Booker has become a superstar.

June 7–Eight Keys to Having Sustainable Organizational Success

Smart leaders are looking for more than just short-term success. They are looking to implement systems which ensure success year after year after year. Two such leaders are general manager John Lynch and head coach Kyle Shanahan of the San Francisco 49ers. Tim Kawakami of *The Athletic* wrote in a June 2 article

> The 49ers are stable enough that they announced to the world that they've got a new QB selected specifically to replace the incumbent who not long ago led them to the Super Bowl . . . and not only has the locker room remained calm, these days (Jimmy) Garoppolo and (Trey) Lance are working together quite amiably in practices and meetings. . . . This all speaks to the talent that Shanahan and Lynch have brought in, to the character of the locker room, the franchise-wide belief that better days are ahead and especially to the Shanahan/Lynch relationship itself. It's there at the start of every practice. Now,

of course, Shanahan and Lynch have to win games. But they've certainly set up the right environment to win a lot of games, for a lot of years.

From his comments, we get great insights into having sustainable success. The 49ers have created a leadership culture. This culture is demonstrated by the establishment of a leadership pipeline ensuring long-term success.

In many organizations, quality depth would cause strife and dysfunction. Players would become selfish because of limited opportunities. A scarcity mindset sets in. But with the 49ers, everyone in the locker room remained calm, and the two quarterbacks worked well together. Another thing Lynch and Shanahan are doing to ensure long-term success is to constantly bring in new talent. Not only are these additions talented, they must be individuals of high character as well. Talented people with great character are attracted to organizations like the 49ers.

The test of sustainable success is if you actually win games. This will be the ultimate litmus test for the 49ers, Lynch, and Shanahan. But they have certainly positioned themselves to do so.

June 9—HEART

> *"If I had my career to do over again, I would pray God would reveal to me the players who should be on my team because they have heart . . . The heart is the most undervalued thing because you can't see it."* —Coach Keith Madison, National Baseball Director of Score International, Hall of Fame former head baseball coach of twenty-five years with the University of Kentucky where he compiled 737 wins.

Whether you lead an athletic organization, church, business, non-profit, or educational organization, we all want people with *heart*. It is an invaluable attribute of great performers. But as Coach Madison said, the problem with heart is you can't see it. You can't measure it. But you know it when you see it.

Former San Francisco 49ers head coach Steve Mariucci said of bypassing Tom Brady in the NFL Draft, "We didn't open up his chest and look at his heart. We didn't look at that. I don't know if anyone did. And what kind of spine he has, the resiliency, and all the things that are making him really great right now." Even if they did open up his chest and look at his heart, would they have known what they should be looking for? I don't think so.

I have long attempted to quantify a person's *heart*, to find a way not to miss it in others. This past Monday, after hearing Coach Madison and other baseball scouts and coaches, I may have finally found my answers.

These individuals focused on 1 Samuel 16:7 (ESV) which states, *"But the Lord said to Samuel, 'Do not look on his appearance or on the height of his stature, because I have rejected him. For the Lord sees not as man sees: man looks on the outward appearance, but the Lord looks on the heart.'"* They discussed what it means to have *heart* and the value of it.

I took copious notes as different coaches and scouts shared. On the subject of being coachable, Andrew Bartman, director of USA Baseball said, "When someone is coachable, they listen." He then added, "The most successful coaches are the ones who are the most coachable themselves." Chicago White Sox scout Kevin Burrell said, "Look for FAT people. Faithful—Available—Teachable." He also added, "How one manages their 'Time & Calendar' will reflect the condition and priority of their heart."

When asked how coaching and his Christian faith intersected, Coach Madison said, "Consistently in the Word and putting God first in everything I did. That's when I had peace." Former Gardner-Webb head baseball coach Rusty Stroupe added, "Don't compartmentalize. (Don't say) I'm coaching now but will put my Christian hat on when I get off the field."

With over twenty-five years of collegiate head coaching experience and current USA Director of SCORE International, Rick Robinson concluded, "You're always standing for the National Anthem. When standing for the National Anthem, I would pray for people committed to the program which included me sharing Christ as part of the program." He also added later via his Twitter account, "Spend time daily praying for players, future players, and their parents. Asking God to send families that are coachable and receptive to hearing the Gospel message through word and deeds. Also divide current players between godly men who are willing to pray for them individually."

As I listened to these great men and others speak, I built the following composite of what a person with *heart* possesses. When looking for coaches, players, teammates, or new employees with heart, look for people who are SCRAPPY—*Skill, Calling, Rejection, Attitude, Perseverance, Purposeful, Yearn to Learn:*

- Skill—The ability to perform with excellence. Even people with heart need to have talent. There was a reason Rudy never started a game for Notre Dame.
- Calling—This is the thing inside you which proclaims, "This *one* thing I must do!" Mike Linch said, "It's the core of me." He also noted, "David conquered the giant of a disconnected heart."
- Rejection—Remember that time when someone said you weren't good enough, that you didn't measure up? Of course,

you do. This challenged your calling, but you moved forward anyway. Rejection provided clarity. It stripped away all non-essentials. You worked even harder. It limited your choices and spurred the hard work and creativity needed to find solutions.

- Attitude—Attitude determines your altitude. A great attitude separates evenly matched people and closes the gap on those more talented than you. You have a great attitude because you can't believe you get to do what you do every day and couldn't imagine doing anything else.

- Perseverance—Because your calling is so clear, you are willing to pay the price needed for your dream to become reality. Perseverance is developed through difficult and trying times. You become mentally strong and resilient.

- Purposeful—Perseverance and resilience births a focused approach. Your life has meaning and direction. Because you have paid the price for success, there is a single-mindedness to your life. As Coach Stroupe said, "Don't compartmentalize. (Don't say) I'm coaching now but will put my Christian hat on when I get off the field."

- Yearn to Learn—Scrappy people are continual learners. They are humble and seek out all the coaching, teammates, resources, and information needed for success. You can't stop them. They will always find a way. Continual learning helps ensure future success.

If you are looking for people with "heart," look for SCRAPPY people. These are the people you want on your team. You can win when you have SCRAPPY people.

June 19–The Truest Measurement of Leadership Performance

On Thursday, June 3rd at 7:05 PM EST, I sent the email you see below:

From: Brian Dodd <BrianD@injoystewardship.com>
Date: Thursday, June 3, 2021 at 7:05 PM
To: "flyingcoachpodcast@gmail.com" <flyingcoachpodcast@gmail.com>
Subject: Question for Coach Sean McVay for the podcast

Sean,

I consider the Washington Redskins coaching staff from 2010 through 2013 to be this generation's Cleveland Browns's coaching staff from 1991 to 1994 under Bill Belichick in terms of being a cradle of future great coaches.

Can you tell me one thing you learned from Coach Mike Shanahan about creating a winning culture and developing young leaders?

Thanks and I love your podcast!

Brian Dodd from Woodstock, GA

Brian Dodd
Director of New Ministry Partnerships | INJOY Stewardship Solutions

The Flying Coach Podcast is hosted by the NFL Network's Peter Schrager and Los Angeles Rams head football coach Sean McVay. I have been a fan of Coach McVay and his innovative approach to leadership for some time. As noted in the email, one thing I am particularly interested in is the time period of 2010 through 2013 when he was an assistant coach with Washington under the leadership of Super Bowl champion Mike Shanahan. In addition to Coach McVay, the staff also included current NFL head coaches Kyle Shanahan and Matt LaFleur. Thus the question shown above. I have hoped one of the respected football authors I enjoy would write about this period of history and reached out to many about their thoughts. Gary Myers, first instance, once tweeted me that one of Coach Shanahan's assistants would have to first win a Super Bowl. I respect his opinion but am interested in learning the leadership principles from Coach Shanahan and his former staff *now*!

I was on a long drive from Atlanta to southern Alabama on Wednesday, June 9, and listened to that week's edition of the podcast. Then I heard the following words when Schrager was asked what was the first email question of the week: *"This question is from Brian in Woodstock Geogia."* Needless to say, a wave of excitement came over me! Not only was my question selected on a well-known podcast, but I was about to get some of the insights I was looking for. Coach McVay's answers did not disappoint.

"The main thing that stands out about Coach Shanahan is the consistency. It's easy to say, hard to do. The way that define consistency is it is the truest measurement of performance." Think about those words. Consistency is the truest measurement of performance. As Coach McVay pointed out, this is because consistency is hard to do. Reliability, dependability, and availability truly are the greatest leadership abilities. You can always be counted on to show up and provide a certain measurement of performance.

Once you are consistent and understand its value, you then begin to expect consistency in yourself and those you lead. Coach Shanahan certainly did. McVay said, "He was consistent in his standards; he upheld in himself as a leader, as a head coach. He demanded that of the players, and I thought he really demanded that of his coaches." When you are a leader who models and demands consistency, you have a chance to create a winning culture. This culture also has a lasting impact on those who serve in it.

McVay concluded his thoughts on Coach Shanahan by saying, "The consistency and standards that he upheld day-in and day-out is something that I'll forever take with me."

So I leave you with this question, is your leadership marked by consistency in the seven following areas:

1. Self-Leadership
2. Culture
3. Expectations
4. Leading Others
5. Knowing Details
6. Reproducing Yourself
7. Commitment to a Philosophy

These were the areas Mike Shanahan was consistent in. If you do so as well, you are likely to achieve a true measurement of leadership performance yourself.

June 20–Father's Day

The following is a recap of the Father's Day devotion I led for the ministry team I serve on at my home church. On this day, there are definitely a few go-to messages you can give:

- The privilege of being a father.
- The joys of being a father.
- How to leave a godly legacy.
- All the things fathers are doing wrong.

I took a different route, a road less traveled. I chose to look at just a small portion of the qualities Jesus displays as our heavenly Father. My objective was not only to shine the spotlight on Him and give Him glory but also to provide a framework for how the Holy Spirit works in our lives to bless our families. Therefore, I pointed out just seven qualities along with supporting scriptures. The following are seven qualities of godly fathers. First is the quality following by the Bible verse which shows the unique characteristics of God Himself.

- Godly fathers are compassionate and gentle. Psalm 103:13 says, "As a father has compassion on his children, so the Lord has compassion on those who fear him" (NIV).
- Godly fathers instill discipline. Proverbs 3:11–12 teaches us, "My son, do not despise the Lord's discipline, and do not resent his rebuke, because the Lord disciplines those he loves, as a father the son he delights in" (NIV).
- Godly fathers are providers. Matthew writes in 6:26, "Look at the birds of the air; they do not sow or reap or store away in barns, and yet your Heavenly Father feeds them. Are you not much more valuable than they?" (NIV).
- Godly fathers teach the Scriptures. They elevate the importance of the Bible. John 14:23 reminds us, "Anyone who loves me will obey my teaching. My Father will love them, and we will come to them and make our home with them" (NIV).
- Godly fathers are generous. They are not greedy or hold too tightly to their resources. James 1:17 says, "Every good and perfect gift is from above, coming down from the Father of the heavenly lights, who does not change like shifting shadows" (NIV).
- Godly fathers protect their families. Going back to Matthew, He says in 26:53, "Do you think I cannot call on my Father, and he will at once put at my disposal more than twelve legions of angels?" (NIV). And finally,
- Godly fathers point their children to Jesus. Jesus himself brings great clarity by telling us in John 14:6, "Jesus

answered, 'I am the way and the truth and the life. No one comes to the Father except through me" (NIV).

June 27–Nick Saban on Reinforcing the Values of the Organization

On June 24, *The Athletic's* Joe Smith wrote an article on championship cultures. It was one of the most insightful articles I read in 2021.

One of my favorite parts was Alabama head coach Nick Saban discussing how players must reinforce the values of the organization. He said, "I tell guys they have to reinforce the values of the organization to be a leader, have to set a good example, and have to help somebody win. You have to care enough about other people to help them for their benefit, not yours. If they're not willing to do that, this is not a role for them. You can't be on the leadership group and walk into meetings late or miss class. That won't work."

June 28–Sir Alex Ferguson

If you are considered the greatest leader in the history of your industry, then you are someone we should all learn from. Such a person is Sir Alex Ferguson. If you are not familiar Sir Alex, you should be. Sir Alex was appointed manager of Manchester United in November 1986. During his twenty-six years with the club, he won thirty-eight trophies, including thirteen Premier League titles, five FA Cups, and two UEFA Champions League titles. His impact as a manager was of such significance, Ferguson was knighted in the 1999 Queen's Birthday Honours list for his services to the game. Sir Alex is now a highly sought-after speaker and consultant in the areas of management and leadership for major companies around the world and academic institutions, such as Harvard.

In his book *Soccer Men: Profiles of the Rogues, Geniuses, and Neurotics Who Dominate the World's Most Popular Sport*, author Simon Kuper dedicates several chapters to this managerial legend. The following are some of the lessons we learn from this leadership genius:

The greatest leaders identify with their company's brand. In essence, elite leaders become the living embodiments of their organization. As Kuper wrote, "He (Ferguson) gradually absorbed three tenets of United's brand: United teams must attack, the world is against United, and United is more a cause than a soccer club." In essence, elite leaders become keepers of their organizational flame. Leaders like Sir Alex Ferguson also hone their strongest character into a weapon for good. For instance, Ferguson's was his temper. He would find colleagues and then practice yelling at them. He would then ask for feedback asking, "Does that sound okay?"

Successful leaders also know who the influencers are within their organization and cultivate mutually beneficial relationships with them. For instance, as a young manager at St. Mirren, Ferguson was actually fired because he could not get along with the team's chairman. He learned his lesson well. He took it a step further by not only learning from those with significant levels of influence, but he learned how to gather helpful information from anyone at any level. Ferguson cultivated as many relationships as possible. Kuper noted, "the three main qualities required for leadership: Control. Managing change. And observation." Ferguson knew everything about Manchester United up to and including the players' dietary habits.

Part of Ferguson's leadership genius was also his ability to manage stress. He simply did not let other people add stress to his life. When people brought problems to Ferguson, his favorite reply was, "I think you can resolve this yourself." Another strength of Ferguson was his skill at handling chaos. All storms have one thing in common, they eventually end. Ferguson was firm on his strategy. He never adjusted it because of crises because he knew they would eventually pass.

Finally, Ferguson had a healthy discontent. He was always unsatisfied. Satisfaction can be fatal to elite leaders. Ferguson said, "The sweetest moment for me is the last minute of victory. After that it drains away quickly. The memory's gone in half an hour." The memory of success may be gone in thirty minutes, but Ferguson's leadership lessons are timeless.

July 3–Shohei Ohtani

Last evening, Los Angeles Angels star DH and pitcher Shohei Ohtani hit two home runs, making him the first player to reach thirty this year. The season he is having is unprecedented. Ohtani is accomplishing things on a baseball field that have not been done since Babe Ruth 100 years ago. After the game, the team's manager Joe Maddon was asked to describe Ohtani. In true Disney fashion, he said, "Maybe supercalifragilisticexpialidocious. Every time he swings the bat, it looks like it could be a home run. He has the patience to draw a walk and then is a really aggressive and astute base runner. And then he pitches. He's always prepared and under control. It's an All-Star performance above and beyond."

Ohtani stands 6'4", throws 101 miles per hour, and consistently hits 470 feet home runs. The twenty-six-year-old player from Iwate Prefecture, Japan is an athletic marvel. Recently, *The Athletic's* Rustin Dodd profiled the international sensation. His article teaches us much about the qualities of Apex Leaders. Great leaders see things and do things average leaders do not. On April 26, Ohtani was the team's starting pitcher against the Texas Rangers while also leading the American League in home runs. The last time this was done was by Ruth on June 13, 1921. You read that right—forty-eight days from being exactly 100 years. No one had accomplished that feat in a century!

Ohtani does many things well but still focuses on his strengths. During that same game, he struck out nine Rangers in five innings, had two hits, two RBIs, and scored three runs. Maddon pointed out the obvious, "A pretty complete game of baseball." He has also earned the respect of his peers. Teammate Justin Upton called Ohtani, "most talented player I've ever seen." Mets starter Marcus Stroman referred to him as "mythical legend in human form." He has even used video games to build relationships with teammates. Like all great leaders, Ohtani ruthlessly self-evaluates. After hitting twenty-two home runs as a rookie in 2018, injuries and other issues resulted in subsequent seasons which did not meet Ohtani's personal expectations. His self-evaluation of his performance was "pathetic."

However, everyone can get better with coaching. In 2018's spring training, Ohtani visited Japanese hitting legend Ichiro Suzuki who helped him change his hitting form. Rather than doing a front leg kick, he now simply does a toe tap. Soliciting feedback has long been one of Ohtani's strengths. Nippon-Ham Fighters former teammate Michael Crotta said of an eighteen-year-old Ohtani, "He was not afraid to speak about what he was doing or how he found success or where he struggled." This continual search for knowledge has made Ohtani a forward-thinking athlete. For instance, he uses the Harada Method, a self-improvement technique focused on writing your goals down, constantly taking notes, and recording the lessons learned. He has also utilized innovative swimming techniques to strengthen his body.

All of this is done with one goal squarely in mind. Former manager Brad Ausmus said, "He wants to be the greatest baseball player ever. So he does everything he can to try and achieve that goal."

Former Angels GM Billy Eppler said, "He wants mastery and he's going to stop at nothing." Leaders like Ohtani are outliers. They are rare and hard to find. Maddon said, "This is a unique athlete, and none of us have been there before." We are watching something historic in Shohei Ohtani.

July 10—Black Widow

In the latest installment of the Marvel cinematic universe, the film's evil mastermind is a former KGB agent named Dreykov. Dreykov oversees the Red Room, a training facility for Russian female spies named Widows. However, his muscle is an individual named The Taskmaster. The Taskmaster has the unique ability to watch and then mimic any fighting style. Throughout the movie, the Taskmaster mimics Steve Rogers, Hawkeye, and especially Natasha Romanoff herself. As I watched *Black Widow*, I was reminded of an important leadership lesson and a story from when my daughter Anna was two years old. During that period of my life, if I had to repeat myself I would say, "Let me try this again," and then I would immediately restate the exact same sentence I just said. We would regularly play a cassette tape (remember those) of Barney the Dinosaur songs while in the car for Anna's enjoyment. One day while taking a family drive, my wife Sonya and I were having a casual conversation. Anna said from her car seat, "I want to hear some Barney music." Sonya and I just continued our conversation when Anna emphatically blurted out, "Let me try this again, I want to hear some Barney music!"

I was immediately reminded that leaders (especially parents) are always being watched and mimicked. I never said, "Let me try this again" again. But what behaviors should leaders wish to model and have replicated in others?

You should want people to see your faith. For example, my fundamental identity is I am a Christian, a child of the one true God, Jesus Christ. I want people to see this reality in my life.

Leaders should also want people to see their love for the Bible. The Bible is God's spoken Word recorded on paper. In its pages are the words of life.

Getting closer to home, leaders should want people to see how they treat their spouse. For me, this shows the priority Sonya has in my life and will dramatically impact Anna's view of whom she will one day marry. Therefore, this has generational implications.

Because of the many demands in their lives, leaders should want to see the priority their family holds. Personally, when I get off work, there is no one I want to spend time with more than my family, and my calendar should reflect this. They are my favorite people.

Speaking of work, leaders should want people to see their work ethic. Never rob your employer by taking more than you have given. In fact, if someone pays you $5, *always* give them $10 worth of value. *Always* arrive early and stay late.

One thing 2020 revealed was how leaders handled crisis. This shows if your faith is real. It is a reminder God is in control and nothing happens He does not cause or allow. Some things in life may hurt *a lot*, but do you trust Him in all things? The year 2020 gave us the wonderful word "pivot." Leaders should want people to see how they handle change. Change is now a constant (and often unwelcome) companion. Never has this statement been more true—Blessed are flexible for they will never be bent out of shape.

What change requires however is the ability to be a continual learner. This is why I place such an importance on reading books.

When Forrest Gump said, "Been there, done that," it was a beloved phrase. However, it is a terrible leadership statement. Leaders should always be going there and doing that.

And one of the things leaders should be showing is generosity and effective ways of managing your money. Leaders should be good and faithful stewards of all entrusted to them. They should be investing and saving. Marketplace leaders should lead the way in paying good and competitive wages. It is also important to build margin in your life to have flexibility to be generous at a moment's notice.

Birds of a feather flock together. Leaders are often known by who they hang around with. Fortunately, I've got a *great* group of friends whom I love dearly. If you are currently looking for a quality group of friends to have in your life, find people you can serve and then ask nothing from them in return. Over time, through your kindness and volunteer efforts, you will accumulate a large network of fellow-minded individuals.

But most important, you want people to see your grace and forgiveness. Life's too short to harbor grudges. The greatest human need is not to be loved, it is to be forgiven. Trust me, I'm not perfect. I need regular forgiveness as much as anyone.

And finally, you want people to see your life and leadership, then have hope. People are dying for hope right now. Here's what I know, if God can bless and use someone like me, He can bless and use anyone.

Leaders, you are always being watched by others. What are they seeing?

July 12–Chris Paul

Wine is not the only thing that gets better with age. Sometimes leaders do as well. Despite previous conflicts with players such as James Harden and Blake Griffin, NBA insiders have long known of the leadership brilliance of Phoenix Suns point guard Chris Paul. Now during this year's NBA season and playoffs, his skills have become apparent to the entire nation. What I also find compelling about Paul's leadership is how much it improved in this, his fifteenth year in the league. It is an indication that even seasoned leaders need to learn new skills and continually adapt their leadership style.

Though he was already a sure-fire first ballot Hall of Famer, playing in the Finals has put Paul in a new historical light. His fiery and sometimes abrasive leadership style has now been redeemed a bit. Also, if the Suns win the title, Paul will be considered the fifth-best point guard of all-time, trailing only Magic Johnson, Steph Curry, Isaiah Thomas, and Oscar Robertson. The title will separate Paul from non-title winners like Allen Iverson, Steve Nash, and others. Paul has gotten even better by continually learning more about the art and craft of leadership. Suns head coach Monty Williams said in a July 6 interview with Jovan Buha of *The Athletic*, "I think you learn over time, leadership is tricky. It's only leadership if people follow you. Otherwise, you're just taking a walk by yourself."

Over the last few seasons, Paul has become much more flexible in terms of how he exercises his leadership. Why you may ask? Paul said, "Experience. Just leadership, experience." For example, in Game 6 of the Western Conference finals, the Los Angeles Clippers had trimmed the Suns's lead to seven points. In the past, the fiery Paul would had engaged his teammates in an extremely elevated fashion. However, this time, he simply led by example, scoring the next eight points by himself and taking the lead back to fifteen points.

Building on the previous point, Coach Williams observed, "I think we both, especially Chris, would tell you he's made adjustments to fit the situation. There are times where he has to tell people directly what the deal is, and then there are times where I've seen him lead in a different way than he did eleven years ago." Paul has learned what other smart leaders also know: it is more important to be effective than right. This is especially true when communicating with others. How you deliver the message is often as important as the message itself. Coach Williams added, "It's better to be effective than right. Sometimes when you're in leadership positions, if you feel like you have to be right all the time, you're probably going to be by yourself, trying to figure out ways to be effective and bring everybody along with you. It can serve you well, and that's what I've seen with him."

Paul has also built bridges with the younger players on the team. He has developed a solid connection with Cam Payne and young stars Deandre Ayton and Devin Booker. Payne said, "When C got here, C taught us a lot. So when he gets to talking, everybody feels like, you know, OK, everybody's holding each other accountable. I think it's the accountability thing for us and the type of relationships we have with each other that if someone's messing up, 1 through 15 has the right to say something to you because we know each other off the court. So, no one ever takes it the wrong way." Paul added, "It's a fun group to be around. And when you're around a group like that, you want to win. You don't ever want the season to end because you actually like being around each other."

The most successful leaders prioritize connecting with the organization's top producers. I mentioned earlier in the book that Devin Booker was a star. In fact, he has become a superstar! Paul has made a special point to befriend Booker, who is also happens to be his neighbor. Booker said of his relationship with Paul, "There's zero ego involved. I think that's the most important part. We both want to see each other succeed. We both want the team to succeed. We all want the team to succeed. So when you're all on the same page that way, the relationships tend to happen. We spend a lot of time together."

Booker added, "This is our first year playing together, so I appreciate him a lot. I've been a sponge to him since the day he got here, before that, but our relationship definitely took off since he's been here."

Paul did not just bring out the best in Booker. His presence also made Ayton, the team's young center, better. He said the addition of Paul was "the best thing that happened to my career." One of the best things Paul gave Ayton was accountability. Ayton continued, "Everything that Chris tells me or tells me what to do, it's from the heart. That dude loves to compete. If you're a real competitor, you're not just listening to how somebody's saying it. You're just getting the message that we're going to get this done. That's the type of relationship we have."

What is one thing you learned from Chris Paul which will make you a better leader? For me as a fifty-five-year-old leader, it was the need to continually adapt my style to connect with top producers!

Note—all quotes came from the aforementioned July 6 article from *The Athletic*.

July 13—Solo Cups

Do you have a great idea right now? In fact, you may have an idea so great you have already acted on it. However, it does not seem to be gaining any traction. Should you give up on it? And if so, when? 400,000-plus people annually post pictures of themselves holding a Solo cup. It is as important to have at parties and family functions as your favorite snack or beverage. Solo cups are so popular that in 2012, Dart Container purchased the product/company for $1 billion. So how did this product become so ubiquitous?

In the 1910s, over 100 years ago, the city of Chicago banned "common drinking cups" because of the germs they were known to spread. However, approximately twenty years later, Leo Hulseman left what would be known as the Dixie Cup Company and started his own business called Paper Container Manufacturing. He would begin selling paper drinking cones. As any entrepreneur knows, he needed equipment to manufacture his product. He purchased a machine from a Czechoslovakian immigrant named George Method Merta, which automatically made the paper cones. George's wife Bozena then made a suggestion which changed the industry forever. She recommended calling the products "solo" cups because you could only use them once.

We now look on Hulseman's idea as genius, but it did not begin that way. If fact, it was approximately forty years later, in the 1970s, before Leo's son, Robert, launched the plastic cup we all know and love today. And the rest, as they say, is partying history! Here's the leadership lesson:

Great leaders are almost always great thinkers as well. One of the things great thinkers have are great ideas. But not all ideas are immediate successes. Thomas Edison received the patent for the light bulb on January 27, 1880, after much trial and error. A reporter asked, "How did it feel to fail 10,000 times?" Edison replied, "I haven't failed. I just found 10,000 ways that won't work." The idea of artificial light was an idea Edison knew was worth holding onto. Here are some things you should know about great ideas:

1. Great ideas lead to other great ideas;
2. Great ideas are often birthed in solitude but mature in collaboration with others;
3. Great ideas are only great if they benefit others;
4. Great ideas need a great plan to be fully-realized; and
5. Great ideas are sustainable, so don't give up on them.

Do you have an idea as great as artificial light or solo cups? Are you perplexed as to why your idea hasn't scaled exponentially? Here is what Leo Hulseman and Thomas Edison would tell you—stay with it! Don't give up on your idea! It may just change the world.

July 17—The Giannis Block

If you have a problem with not focusing on the present, or are too preoccupied with the past, the following words are for you. With 1:23 left to go in Game 4 of the NBA Finals and the Milwaukee Bucks clinging to a 101–99 lead over the Phoenix Suns, Suns point guard Chris Paul brought the ball down the court for the potential tying or go-ahead basket. The ensuing play resulted in Devin Booker throwing a lob pass for a certain Deandre Ayton dunk. However, out of nowhere, two-time NBA MVP Giannis Antetokounmpo came out of seemingly nowhere to block the dunk attempt. His effort resulted in what is now considered one of the top three defensive plays in NBA Finals history. Giannis's block helped secure the team's victory and tie the series at 2–2. In the post-game news conference, Giannis gave his thoughts on the play. From his thoughts we learn a number of life-changing leadership lessons every leader can apply.

Trust your training in high-pressure situations
Giannis said, "It's incredible what your body is [able] to do." As you develop deep practice habits and muscle memory, your training will take over in difficult situations. When it does, trust it.

We also learn the difference between successful and unsuccessful people is executing in high-pressure situations. Tom Brady once said, "To me what separates really good players from great players—execute well under pressure. The biggest game. The biggest stage. That's what playing quarterback is all about." The same is true with leadership and basketball. Giannis added, "When you think about winning, you go to the extreme." Great leaders simply find a way while others make excuses.

Smart leaders know to let your past inform you, your present instruct you, and your future inspire you. The past is simply a data point. It should give you confidence and/or instruction but your focus as a leader needs to be on what is next. Giannis noted, "I got to move on. I got to keep making winning plays. I got to keep competing. I got to keep finding ways to help my team be great. Great moment. I appreciate the moment. Great moment. [But] we got to move on." So do you as a leader.

Giannis then provided the leadership quote of the year. It is so profound that each portion of the statement will stand alone.

Your Ego Focuses on the Past
Yesterday ended last night. A leader's windshield (what lies ahead) should always be larger and more pronounced than your rearview mirror (what's in the past). As Babe Ruth said, "Yesterday's home run won't win today's game." Giannis would have liked The Babe. He said, "I cannot explain the play. But, at the end of the day, that's in the past. When you talk about the past, that's your ego talking. It's in the past. It's over with."

Your Pride Predicts the Future

Leaders are not promised anything in the future. The future is an opportunity which must be seized. Giannis understands this. He said, "I figured out a mindset to have that when you focus on the past, that's your ego. I did this. We were able to beat this team 4–0. I did this in the past. I won that in the past.' When I focus on the future, it's my pride. 'Yeah, next game, Game 5, I (will) do this and this and this. I'm going to dominate.' That's your pride talking. It doesn't happen. You're right here."

Your Humility Focuses on the Moment

As mentioned earlier, your ego focuses on the past. Your pride predicts the future. But your humility allows you to focus on the moment. Your humility allows you to be where your feet are and to be in the moment. Giannis said, "I kind of try to focus on the moment, in the present. That's humility. That's being humble. That's not setting no [sic] expectation. That's going out there, enjoying the game, competing at a high level."

But being in the moment often requires accountability. As talked about in the opening paragraph, we are a distracted society. We have so many options and so many messages coming at us, it is hard to stop, focus, and concentrate. Many of us need help doing so. Giannis acknowledged, "I think I've had people throughout my life that helped me with that." If the two-time NBA MVP needs help, perhaps you and I do as well.

Finally, we learn focus is a skill that can be mastered. Great leaders make no excuses. You can beat the problem of distraction. Giannis concluded, "But that is a skill that I've tried to, like, kind of . . . master it. It's been working so far, so I'm not going to stop." Focus is not just a state of mind; it is a skill. And skills can be mastered.

July 18—Twenty Questions to Determine Pastoral Trust

I am reminded of the following two passages which provide the biblical qualifications of a pastor. Please note the word *elder* is the same Greek word as *pastor.* Titus 1:5–9 (ESV) teaches:

> *This is why I left you in Crete, so that you might put what remained into order, and appoint elders in every town as I directed you—if anyone is above reproach, the husband of one wife, and his children are believers and not open to the charge of debauchery or insubordination. For an overseer, as God's steward, must be above reproach. He must not be arrogant or quick-tempered or a drunkard or violent or greedy for gain, but hospitable, a lover of good, self-controlled, upright, holy, and disciplined. He must hold firm to the trustworthy word as taught, so that he may be able to give instruction in sound doctrine and also to rebuke those who contradict it.*

Likewise, 1 Timothy 3:1–7 (ESV) states:

> *The saying is trustworthy: If anyone aspires to the office of overseer, he desires a noble task. Therefore an overseer must be above reproach, the husband of one wife, soberminded, self-controlled, respectable, hospitable, able to teach, not a drunkard, not violent but gentle, not quarrelsome, not a lover of money. He must manage his own household well, with all dignity keeping his children submissive, for if someone does not know how to manage his own household, how will he care for God's church? He must not be a recent convert, or he may become puffed up with conceit and fall into the condemnation of the devil. Moreover, he must be well*

thought of by outsiders, so that he may not fall into disgrace, into a snare of the devil.

From these two passages, we can build a biblical framework for not only the qualifications of a pastor, but whether they are trustworthy in fulfilling their responsibilities in these areas and therefore worth following. As a result, pastoral trust can be measurable. I offer this self-assessment as a loving tool to help pastors not get blindsided by trust issues and also proactively identify areas to work on. With each question below, pastors can score themselves in the area of trust.

Now let's take the self-assessment. Give yourself 1 to 5 points for each question based upon the following grid:

- 5 Points—Completely Trustworthy. Above Reproach.
- 4 Points—Trustworthy. You are well-above average in this area.
- 3 Points—Somewhat Trustworthy. You have had some wins and losses in this area.
- 2 Points—Not Trustworthy. There is much work to do in this area.
- 1 Points—Completely Untrustworthy. There are multiple broken promises and missed expectations in this area.

The following are the questions. Once again, give yourself a score of 1 to 5 in each area.

1. Is the pastor devoted to his wife? In other words, is he a one-woman man?
2. Are the pastor's children under submission? They won't be perfect, but a pastor's first flock is his family.
3. Is the pastor a faithful steward of God's resources?

4. Is the pastor humble? Does he apologize to individuals and the congregation when necessary?
5. Is the pastor gentle? Does he anger easily and abuse others with his quick-temper?
6. Does the pastor drink or struggle with alcohol?
7. Is the pastor a peacemaker?
8. Is the pastor forthright with all his financial dealings? Is he greedy? Does he struggle with money?
9. Is the pastor hospitable? Does he open his home and make it a place for ministry?
10. Does the pastor love what is good and hate what is evil?
11. Is the pastor self-controlled? In particular, does the pastor have self-control in the areas of diet, time, speech, exercise, relationships, sex, humor, and money?
12. Is the pastor upright? Does the pastor have integrity in how he treats others?
13. Does the pastor prioritize personal holiness over personal pleasure?
14. Can the pastor teach, utilizing sound doctrine? Does the pastor preach fearlessly? Can the pastor deliver hard truths? Is the pastor a false teacher?
15. Is the pastor spiritually mature?
16. Is the pastor respectable? In other words, are there any witnesses to a sinful lifestyle the pastor may have?
17. Is the pastor an example to the flock? Pastors should be biblical examples in the areas of sexuality, time management, marriage, parenting, worship, relationships, and any other way. A pastor should be a picture of the desired destination in which others should wish to arrive.
18. Has the pastor broken promises to individuals or the congregation in the past? Has the pastor done what he said he would do? Have goals been met or achieved?

19. Does the pastor surround himself with people who are respectable and trustworthy? Also, does the pastor's inner circle trust him?
20. Is the pastor's vision worth following?

Now add up your totals. The following are things you now need to know.

- 90 to 100 Points—You have an incredible amount of trust. This is a gift and God has blessed you. Protect and steward it well. Love your people because they love you.
- 80 to 89 Points—You have a lot of trust. Great job! Rejoice, but don't get overconfident. Work on the areas which have revealed themselves to potentially erode trust.
- 70 to 79 Points—You have a certain level of trust, but you will need to borrow the trust of others to advance any ministry agenda. Many new pastors may fall in this area because they simply have not had enough time to start getting wins under their belt.
- Below 70 Points—You likely do not have the influence necessary to advance any ministry initiative. People are likely leaving the church. Staff turnover is a constant. Repentance and apologies are in order.

How did you score? What does this tell you about your next steps as a leader?

I want to thank the Acts 29 organization, which added much of the context to the assessment.

July 24—Thirteen Components of a Winning Culture

In November 2002, Theo Epstein was hired as the general manager of the Boston Red Sox. During his tenure, Epstein was credited with breaking "The Curse of the Bambino" as the team won the 2004 and 2007 World Series championships. These were the first World Series titles for the Red Sox since 1918 when the team infamously traded Babe Ruth to the New York Yankees. As a result, Epstein is a true legend in the New England area. On October 12, 2011, Epstein left the Red Sox to become the president of the Chicago Cubs. Epstein took out a full-page ad in *The Boston Globe* to expressing his appreciation to the Red Sox fans. The following is an excerpt from his letter:

> *Beyond the results on the field, I believe the Red Sox came to stand for certain things over the last decade. Pride in the uniform. Appreciation of our history. Controlling the strike zone. Grinding at-bats. Having each other's backs. Rising to the moment. Never backing down. Connection to the fans. Hard work. Playing with passion and urgency. These concepts were taught in the minor leagues and reinforced at the big-league level by our homegrown players by Tito (Francona), a selfless leader who always put the Red Sox first. These principles united the organization and came to define us.*

This portion of the letter is all about the culture Epstein had created with the Red Sox. His thoughts give us a picture into the components of a winning culture. A winning culture has symbols. This is part of your brand and the ethos you have created. This is what people think of when they hear you or your organization's name. Epstein said, "Pride in the uniform." He understood it meant something to an entire region when you put on the Red Sox jersey.

A winning culture has history and a sense of responsibility to those who came before you. You are standing on the shoulders of others who built the foundation you now operate on. There is a responsibility implied here. Epstein added, "Appreciation of our history."

A winning culture is disciplined. This speaks to focus and single-mindedness. Epstein noted the expectation of the players was "Controlling the strike zone. Grinding at-bats." Your culture is greatly impacted by the lonely work, the things which do not receive public applause, that your team does.

A winning culture has accountability. We are our brother's keeper. Winning cultures are not made up of individual contractors. There is a sense of mutual responsibility. Epstein said it this way, "Having each other's backs."

A winning culture embraces the privilege of pressure. Leaders of winning cultures understand pressure comes with winning. Welcome or not, it is one of its rewards. There is no pressure with average or below-average cultures. Jurgen Klopp, the manager of the Liverpool futbol team, said, "The higher you climb performance-wise, the more likely it gets you'll have a stressful conclusion of the season." Epstein understands this and expects the Red Sox to be *rising to the moment.*

A winning culture is resilient. Building a winning culture is not easy. There are constant roadblocks and challenges to overcome. Failure is a constant companion. For example, when you read the Bible, you will learn God never called anyone to an easy task or assignment. Therefore, a primary component of a winning culture is "never backing down." Mental toughness is a requirement in winning cultures.

A winning culture builds community among its members. They are highly inclusive. People want to be a part of them. The Red Sox are a picture of the New England region. Epstein acknowledged what all baseball fans know, and that is the team's "Connection to the fans." Klopp would agree with Epstein. He added, "We are not alone on this planet, and we should not be alone in a futbol stadium."

A winning culture works hard, very hard. Hard work works. You cannot have a winning team without it. Laziness is not present in winning cultures. It is simply not tolerated. Basketball announcer and former coach Jeff Van Gundy says, "Your best player has to set a tone of intolerance for anything that gets in the way of winning." Epstein did not want this to be assumed. He proclaimed the Red Sox will be characterized by "Hard work."

A winning culture is easily recognizable. It has passion and a sense of urgency. Passion is many things, but ultimately it is owning the result. Passion also has a sense of immediacy. This was indicative of the Red Sox during the Epstein era. He expected the team to be "Playing with passion and urgency."

A winning culture continually reinforces itself at all levels of the organization by the language it uses. Your culture will develop either by default or design. The tenants of your organization must be taught, modeled, and repeated over and over again. Epstein said, "These concepts were taught in the minor leagues and reinforced at the big-league level by our homegrown players."

A winning culture is a picture of its leader. Your culture is the length and shadow of a single individual—the leader. If you want a better culture, get a better leader and the Red Sox had a great one. Epstein added to the previous statement by recognizing the team's manager, "These concepts were taught in the minor leagues and reinforced at the big-league level by our homegrown players by Tito (Francona), a selfless leader who always put the Red Sox first."

A winning culture unites your organization. Epstein summarized his thoughts by saying, "These principles united the organization." That's what winning cultures do. They bring people together and create a sense of togetherness. Finally, a winning culture defines your organization. Epstein concluded, "and came to define us."

After leaving the Red Sox, Theo Epstein proved once again to be one of the great culture builders of all-time. As president of the 2016 Chicago Cubs, he led the team to its first World Series championship in 108 years, removing the "Curse of the Billy Goat."

July 29–Nick Saban's Eight Benefits to Being on a Team

This Halloween, Nick Saban, the legendary head football coach of the Alabama Crimson Tide, will celebrate his seventieth birthday. He has had quite a twenty-six-year coaching career. The following are just a list of his numerous accomplishments at the time of this writing:

- Seven national championships;
- Nine Southeastern Conference championships;
- Numerous Coach of the Year awards;
- 261–65–1 overall college record (.800);
- 170–23 record at Alabama (.881);
- After six players were selected in the first round of the 2021 NFL Draft, Coach Saban has coached thirty-nine first rounders while at Alabama—and counting. Overall, he has coached forty-four first rounders.

But probably most importantly, on December 18, Coach Saban will celebrate his fiftieth wedding anniversary to Ms. Terry. Well done!

Coach Saban is clearly a success on and off the field. But there is something he fears. On July 20, Coach Saban was the keynote speaker at the eighty-ninth annual Texas High School Coaches Association convention. As reported by *The Athletic*'s Sam Kahn, Jr., Coach Saban said "I played second base in Little League when I was nine years old. I've been a part of a team since I was nine years old. That's sixty years I've been a part of a team. I am scared to death of when I'm not going to be a part of a team."

To give you some insight into his thoughts, Coach Saban added, "I want to be a part of a team. It's a great experience to try to get people to work together, get people to buy into the principles and values of your organization, and to each other, and to the standard that you have to get them to do it so that they can have success, so that together they can have success. It's a great challenge. I enjoy it."

Coach Saban teaches us in his comments a number of things about being on a winning team. When you're on a winning team, you are not alone. You are part of a group of people who work together. You have a shared system of beliefs and behaviors. There is accountability. You experience joy and pain together. Ironically, you can still have individual success, but you also get the thrill which can only come from the collective success of a team. Now you know why Coach Saban would miss being part of a team.

August 1–Alaskan Bear Attack

Nome, Alaska, is a remote town with a population of 3,866, located on the southern Seward Peninsula of the Bering Sea. It is known for being the most famous gold rush town in the state during the early 1900s. The city is so remote it is not part of Alaska's roadway system. The most common way to get there is a ninety-minute flight from Anchorage. Now go about forty miles from Nome further into the wilderness to an abandoned mining camp, and this is where you would have found Richard Jessee in early July. Jessee was surely enjoying the solitude and breathtaking scenery of the Alaskan wilderness. However, the wilderness of Alaska, while beautiful and quite peaceful, can also be a very challenging and extremely dangerous place.

One day, Jessee's ATV was crossing a river, towing a trailer, when suddenly, he was ambushed by a grizzly bear. The ATV, trailer, and most importantly his cell phone all sank to the bottom of the river. Jessee used his gun to escape, but he was alone, stranded, and afraid as he tried to survive being attacked by the most dangerous land mammal in the world forty miles from the nearest town. He was then terrorized and stalked for several days as the bear kept returning. Miraculously, on July 16, a Coast Guard helicopter flying from Kotzbue to Nome was forced off course and had to maneuver around low clouding. It was then Lieutenant A.J. Hammac saw an SOS sign on top of a shack. He later said, "We don't really come across people in the middle of nowhere. He was kind of struggling. When we came around, he was on his hands and knees waving a white flag." Lt. Commander Jared Carbajal added, "(My co-pilot) said, 'Hey, there's a guy down there, and he's waving at us.'" I said, "Is he waving with one hand or two hands?" Well, that's usually a sign of distress.

From there the helicopter descended and rescued Jessee. He was then taken to an emergency medical facility in Nome where he is expected to make a full recovery. I'm sure the book and movie deals are already being negotiated. Until then, there are several leadership lessons we can learn from this harrowing tale. We are at our best (and most safe) when working in a team environment.

Human beings were not made to be in solitude for extended periods of time. Being alone opens us up for spiritual, emotional, psychological, and in the case of Richard Jessee, physical attack.

As we just discussed, being part of a team makes us better. We are more effective. When you are part of a team, there are people who will watch your back. Also, they have resources which, when applied appropriately, will help you tremendously. Simply put, you can accomplish more with "we" than you can with "me." Don't face life or leadership alone. You are not likely to survive.

Use clear, crisp, and compelling communication during times of crisis. SOS is only three letters but packs significant meaning. During times of crisis, it is important to use an economy of words. Extended elaborations during stressful situations cause frustration and confusion. SOS is clear (HELP!), crisp (three letters), and compelling (a distress signal). Its message resulted in immediate action once seen.

Don't quit. Who knows what the clouds will bring in. We have institutionalized quitting in our world today and often even celebrate it. As a result, we are beginning to see a deficit of mental toughness. Three of the most important leadership abilities are reliability, availability, and dependability. Jessee's commitment to survive the attacking grizzly for several days reminded me of Tom Hanks playing the role of Chuck Noland, FedEx employee, in the wonderful movie *Castaway*.

Recounting his experience while stranded on an island with no hope of rescue, Nolad said, "I knew I had to stay alive. Somehow I had to keep breathing even though there was no reason to hope. And all my logic said I would never see this place again. So that's what I did. I stayed alive. I kept breathing. And one day that logic was proven all wrong because the tide came in. It gave me a sail . . . I've got to keep breathing because tomorrow the sun will rise. Who knows what the tide could bring."

Richard Jessee also stayed alive as well. He kept breathing. The sun continued to rise over the Alaskan wilderness. And one day, low cloud cover came in. He was rescued. Who knew what the clouds would bring in.

If you are thinking of quitting your leadership responsibilities, *don't!* The same could happen for you.

August 14–David's Mighty Men

The following are the words recorded in 1 Samuel 23:8–17 (ESV) as David was hiding in exile from King Saul:

> *These are the names of the mighty men whom David had: Josheb-basshebeth a Tahchemonite; he was chief of the three.[a] He wielded his spear[a] against eight hundred whom he killed at one time.*
>
> *9 And next to him among the three mighty men was Eleazar the son of Dodo, son of Ahohi. He was with David when they defied the Philistines who were gathered there for battle, and the men of Israel withdrew. 10 He rose and struck down the Philistines until his hand was weary, and his hand clung to the sword. And the Lord brought about a great victory that day, and the men returned after him only to strip the slain.*
>
> *11 And next to him was Shammah, the son of Agee the Hararite. The Philistines gathered together at Lehi,[a] where there was a plot of ground full of lentils, and the men fled from the Philistines. 12 But he took his stand in the midst of the plot and defended it and struck down the Philistines, and the Lord worked a great victory.*

¹³ And three of the thirty chief men went down and came about harvest time to David at the cave of Adullam, when a band of Philistines was encamped in the Valley of Rephaim. ¹⁴ David was then in the stronghold, and the garrison of the Philistines was then at Bethlehem. ¹⁵ And David said longingly, "Oh, that someone would give me water to drink from the well of Bethlehem that is by the gate!" ¹⁶ Then the three mighty men broke through the camp of the Philistines and drew water out of the well of Bethlehem that was by the gate and carried and brought it to David. But he would not drink of it. He poured it out to the Lord ¹⁷ and said, "Far be it from me, O Lord, that I should do this. Shall I drink the blood of the men who went at the risk of their lives?" Therefore he would not drink it. These things the three mighty men did.

After reading the verses above, we learn the four qualities you need from those who make up your inner circle:

Production
From Josheb-basshebeth, we learn production. He once killed 800 enemy personnel with only a spear! Wow! This great warrior produced an extraordinary amount of results. He simply got the job done in a *big* way! What is also embedded in his level of production was incredible physical stamina, mastery of his skill, and superior efficiency.

Passion
From Eleazar, we learn passion. As David's men were about to fight the Philistines, it says they withdrew. In other words, the men ran away—except for Eleazar. He fought until he was weary, but he owned the result. He had a "not on my watch" type of mentality.

And after personally delivering victory, it says they literally had to pry his sword out of his hand. That's passion.

Perseverance

From Shammah, we learn perseverance. When there was another conflict with the Philistines over a plot of ground at Lehi, once again, everyone ran except for Shammah. When things got tough, he stood his ground. He did not run. Shammah did not shrink from the challenge; he pressed into it. As a result, he struck down their entire army, and the Lord worked a great victory through him.

Loyalty

Finally, when David longed for the refreshing waters from the well of Bethlehem, these three men collectively risked their lives by crossing into enemy territory to get this water for their leader. From these men, we learn loyalty. They loved David and would do anything to serve him. While loyalty may not make you a leader, disloyalty will definitely disqualify you as one.

As you look as those closest to you, do they possess the qualities of production, passion, perseverance, and loyalty? If not, it may be time to change your inner circle.

August 16—Who Is Responsible for Maintaining Culture in Your Organization?

Jenni Catron, Founder and CEO of The 4Sight Group, recently said, *"Culture is the engine that makes vision a reality."* I agree with Jenni, but the question then begs—who then is driving and maintaining the vehicle the engine resides in?

Steph Curry is a superstar. He is a two-time Most Valuable Player for the Golden State Warriors, a four-time All-NBA first-team selection, played in seven NBA All-Star games, and won three

NBA championships. Curry is the face of the franchise and one of the faces on the league. And he is paid as such. On August 6, Curry signed a four-year, $215 million contract extension with the club. It is the second $200-plus million contract of his career. But a player of his caliber has options, and there was speculation Curry could play elsewhere at the conclusion of his current deal.

Responding to those rumors, he noted, "It's one of those things where you set your priority list on how you want to go about it and what's really important. That takes some time to really identify. Once you do, for me at least, all those other kinds of fantasies about playing somewhere else, whatever squad it would be with and who it would be with, kind of goes out the door, knowing the culture that we built here. So it's on me to maintain that culture." Steph Curry gives insight into one of the most important questions any organization must answer if it wishes to have a healthy and winning culture—who is the person most responsible for maintaining the culture of the organization?

The answer is the leader.

Now yes, Steph Curry has a head coach, a general manager, and an ownership group. But leadership is influence, not position. Curry has the wisdom, insight, institutional knowledge, and sense of personal responsibility to know it's on him as the team's best player to maintain the culture. To repeat Jeff Van Gundy's statement, "Your best player must set the intolerance for anybody who gets in the way of winning." That person, the engine of the Golden State Warriors who makes vision reality, is Steph Curry.

Who is the engine for your organization? What is their level of intolerance for non-performance? This is the responsibility and ownership of the culture that comes with being the leader. Two of the oldest leadership axioms are so goes your leader, so goes the people, and the speed of your leader is the speed of the team. If you want a better culture, get a better leader. Go find a leader like Steph Curry.

August 17—The Difference Between Healthy and Unhealthy Relationships

I was recently volunteering at a leadership conference and speaking with one of event's organizers. We were having a very pleasant conversation, and she expressed her gratefulness for my participation. I replied, "Well, I'm just trying to earn my free ticket!"

She then said, "We could never pay you back for all you given us." My sheepish response was, "I could *never* pay *you* back for you given me."

As the day progressed I thought about that exchange quite often. Then I had the following insight: *If you think you could never pay me back for all I given you, and I think I could never pay you back for all you given me, we are going to have a very healthy relationship.*

Relationships become unhealthy when one or both of the parties feel they are giving far more than they are getting in return. Over time, this relationship will end because it simply becomes counter-productive for those involved who are feeling used and taken advantage of.

On the same day of this conversation, quarterback Josh Allen of the Buffalo Bills signed a six-year, $253 million contract extension with $150 million guaranteed. I know this is the market rate for a quarterback of Allen's caliber but I couldn't help but think: What would Josh Allen have to do for the Bills' owner Terry Pegula and the team's executives for them to say to him, "We could never pay you back for all you giving us," while simultaneously have Josh

Allen say, "I know it was the market rate, but I could never pay you back for all given me." Something tells me only a Super Bowl will do.

How many relationships do you currently have, personal and professional, which you would consider healthy?

August 18–Kevin Durant

Many leaders I know are blessed with God-given talent. They are smart, charismatic, uniquely skilled, well-educated, and seemingly have all the potential in the world. But many did not reach their potential. Why?

On August 7, the United States Olympics men's basketball team won the gold medal by defeating Spain 87–82. The Americans were led by Kevin Durant who scored a team-high twenty-nine points. During the games, Durant further cemented a claim to being the world's best player by becoming America's all-time Olympic scoring leader with 435 points in twenty-two games. In addition to his three Olympic gold medals, the following are a list of just some of his current NBA career accomplishments:

- 2007–2008 Rookie of the Year
- 2013–2014 NBA Most Valuable Player
- Two NBA championships
- Two-time Finals Most Valuable Player
- Eleven All-Star games
- Two-time All-Star game Most Valuable Player
- Four-time NBA scoring champ
- 23,883 career points

Durant is an uber-talented player who has exceeded the potential spotted in him as a teenager. But while he is blessed physically at

6'10" (some say he is a seven-footer) with incredible athleticism and shooting guard skills, it is his work ethic which is noteworthy. Durant's former head coach while in Oklahoma City, Scott Brooks, said, "He works each day like he's trying to make the team." What does working each day like you're trying to make the team look like? Well, it starts by showing up, going to work every day and often putting in extra hours. It is doing the lonely work, the work know one sees but shows up at critical times. This type of work is humble, not entitled, and does not take shortcuts.

People trying to make the team have a great attitude. In other words, they play well with others and get along with people. They put the team's goals ahead of their own. Hard workers are continual learners and respond well to coaching. But most importantly, they outwork their talent and become the embodiment of the culture you wish to create.

In closing, I have two questions for you. First, are you as a leader maximizing your God-given talent? If not, what is one thing you learned from Kevin Durant which will help you do so?

August 19–*What If?*

Currently Disney+ is reimagining several Marvel Cinematic Universe storylines in an animated series entitled *What If.* For instance, the initial episode wondered what if Peggy Carter was forced through an unexpected series of events to take the Super Soldier serum rather than Steve Rogers. As a result, she would have become Captain America.

What Disney+ and the MCU are reminding us is one of the most important qualities leaders need to have in the (post) pandemic world is curiosity. Curiosity often reveals itself in leaders who have the ability and humility to ask great questions. And smart leaders have discovered there are few questions better than "What if?"

"What if" gives us new perspectives. It provides new thinking and opens up undiscovered possibilities. This question challenges our assumptions. "What if" unlocks creativity. It creates options. Once again, "What if" is all about the value of curiosity.

Francesca Gina in her excellent book *Rebel Talent: Why It Pays to Break the Rules at Work and Life* cites a study conducted by Spencer Harrison of the INSEAD business school in France. Over a two-week period, salespeople of an e-commerce site were periodically asked to judge their level of curiosity regarding their individual jobs and its company's products on a scale of 1-to-10. What they discovered was fascinating! If their level of curiosity increased by just a single point, or 10 percent (ex. their level or curiosity went from a 6 to a 7), their productivity (i.e., sales numbers) increased 34 percent!

What we learn is, asking "What if" reveals if there is a better way to do something and if we are solving the right problem. Better yet, asking "What if" uncovers what our (prospective) customers' needs are and make it easier to serve them. What if we changed our services, products, or processes to meet ever-changing needs? What if we looked for a different set of skills in the people we hire or developed a new set of relationships? What if we viewed failure differently and rewarded things like innovation? What if we scheduled time to think creatively and tried something new? Furthermore, what if we viewed problems as opportunities for improvement rather than threats?

On a personal level, what if everyone in our organization had a personal growth plan? What if we read more books and viewed decisions as investments rather than expenses? But best yet, what if our best days are ahead? What if we could actually change the world today? Finally, what if we asked God more often what He thinks?

August 22–"This Is Not a Democracy"

Alabama Crimson Tide head coach Nick Saban is famous for using his press conferences to target messages to individual players, the team, the media, the fans, or any other group who needs addressing at a particular moment. Do not be confused; the media and its questions are not driving the flow of information. Coach Saban strategically uses this time to create culture and drive the mission and vision of his organization. After all, it is *his* press conference to get out *his* message, and he brilliantly uses the media to fulfill his purposes. Following Saturday's second team scrimmage, Coach Saban was asked about highly touted tight end Jahleel Billingsley's low status on the depth chart. The question afforded him the opportunity to address issues about authority, the prioritization of practice, and the players creating value for themselves.

One lesson we learned from the press conference was each of us is responsible for our own personal development. Your organization and its culture create the opportunity, but ultimately your success and development is up to you. Regarding Billingsley's position on the depth chart, Saban said, "Well that's up to him. That's not up to me. He knows what he's supposed to do in practice. He knows what he's supposed to do."

From that statement we can conclude it is Coach Saban himself who sets the culture at the University of Alabama. He emphatically said, "You know, this is not a democracy. Everybody doesn't get to do what they want to do. Everybody doesn't get to do what they feel like doing. You've got to buy in and do what you're supposed to do to be a part of the team and do the things you need to do in practice every day." There is no lack of clarity on what is expected from Alabama Crimson Tide athletes. Just in case there was any further confusion, Coach Saban clarified it by saying, "A sense of urgency, play fast, execute, do your job."

Those players who buy-in to the team's culture experience several unique benefits. Mainly, they create value for themselves in the eyes of professional scouts and coaches. Coach Saban continued, "It's a privilege for everybody to go out there and be able to create value for yourself. And we have scouts at practice every day." He concluded, "I try to get them to do it. I try to point out the importance of them doing it, but it's up to them to do it. Maybe that's not my question to answer." In this case, it is Jahleel Billingsley's.

Coach Saban teaches us three primary lessons about creating value for ourselves. First, each of us have an opportunity to create value for ourselves every single day. Regardless of your profession, smart leaders know they are constantly being watched and evaluated. Coach Saban said, "So, everybody thinks it's just about playing in a game. It's not just about playing in the game. They watch practice film; they watch guys every day. You guys on ESPN, you evaluate what happens in the game, but they evaluate what happens every day, what you do every day."

Second, you should be strategic about creating value for yourself. Do you create value for yourself by default or design? You should have a value creation strategy. Coach Saban asked the question I now ask you, "So, what are you doing every day to create any value for yourself?" Finally, creating value for yourself creates confidence in your own ability. Creating value is not all about you. It actually makes you a more useful teammate. Coach Saban insightfully noted, "But you got to create value for yourself so that your teammates and everybody gets confidence in you so that you can have their confidence when you go out there and play, and that's up to every player on the team. I don't make that decision for everybody on the team."

August 28–The Number 1 Asset Leaders Have for Problem Solving

On Sunday, December 7, 1941, the Japanese conducted a surprise aerial attack on the United States naval fleet located at Pearl Harbor on Oahu Island, Hawaii. The following day, President Franklin Delano Roosevelt delivered the speech to Congress asking for a state of war to be declared. His speech would go down in history because of the phrase, "Yesterday, December 7, 1941 a date which will live in infamy." But there is something many people don't know about the speech. There was great concern for the president's safety and how he was going to be transported from the White House to the Capitol building to deliver the address to Congress and the nation. Believe it or not, at the time, federal law prohibited the purchase of any car over $750. (Yes, you read that right!)

However, one of the Secret Service members had a very creative solution. Ten years prior, in 1931, the United States Treasury Department seized a 1928 Cadillac V-8 Town Sedan from the legendary gangster Al Capone for tax evasion. As you would expect, Capone's car was not just any normal Cadillac. It was a car befitting the most famous gangster in American history. This particular vehicle came equipped with the following:

- 3,000 lbs. of armor;
- One-inch-thick bulletproof windows;
- A specially installed siren;
- Flashing lights hidden in the grille; and
- A police scanner (a must-have for any successful gangster).

Bottom line, the travel/safety problem was solved. After conducting a maintenance check to ensure the car would still run properly, President Roosevelt was transported to the capital building in the safest vehicle they could find—Al Capone's Cadillac V-8 Town Sedan.

This brings me to the subject of creativity. Creativity is not skinny jeans that don't reach your ankles, a low v-neck, scarf, Converse shoes, and messed up hair. That is not creativity. That is style. Creativity is the ability to look at the resources you *already* have at your disposal (like Capone's car) and discover new applications of those existing resources to solve problems and advance your organization's mission and vision.

Exodus 4:1–3 records a fascinating exchange between God and Moses:

> *Then Moses answered, "But behold, they will not believe me or listen to my voice, for they will say, 'The Lord did not appear to you.'" The Lord said to him, "What is that in your hand?" He said, "A staff." And he said, "Throw it on the ground." So he threw it on the ground, and it became a serpent, and Moses ran from it. (ESV)*

In other words, Moses had everything he needed for success already in his hand. The United States government already had everything it needed to safely transport President Roosevelt to the Capitol. Whatever problem you may be facing, you already have everything you need as well. Therefore, if you are facing a seemingly insurmountable task, I ask you the same set of questions God asked Moses, "What is that in your hand? What resources do you already have? That's your number 1 asset. How could they be leveraged differently to solve problems? How can what is in your hand advance your mission and vision?"

So if you're facing a problem, get your team together. Get creative. Look around. Do an inventory. Like President Roosevelt, you just might find a ten-year-old resource sitting in your garage which will solve your problem. Fun fact—Capone's car was sold at auction in 2009 for $309,000. It currently sits in Whiskey Pete's Hotel and Casino located thirty-five miles south of Las Vegas.

September 8–Smart Decisions and Bad Decisions

A uniquely gifted Italian man by the name of Ferruccio had a keen interest in mechanics. Prior to World War II, he studied the subject at the famous Fratelli Taddia Technical Institute located about a half-hour from Bologna. After being drafted into the country's Royal Air Force, he served as a mechanic and ultimately became the unit's supervisor. Hard times then fell upon Ferruccio when he became a prisoner of war in 1945. One year later he returned home, but then his wife passed away in 1947. But his love for machinery remained so much so that he developed a particular love for farm equipment. Ferruccio had a creative idea to take discarded military machine parts left over from the war and repurpose them into useful farming tools and machines. He was so successful, he ultimately started his own business selling tractors. The name of his company was Lamborghini Trattori after Ferruccio's last name.

Ferruccio Lamborghini also enjoyed cars. Because of his expert knowledge of machinery, he discovered inefficiencies in the clutches of Ferraris. He brought his findings to Enzo Ferrari himself. Rather than being appreciative for this opportunity to improve his product, the legendary pride of Ferrari led him to dismiss both Lamborghini and his suggestions about the car's clutch. Many people, after experiencing this humiliation, would have gone back to their very successful tractor business and lived the simple life. But not Lamborghini. He started taking those same materials used for tractors and began making cars—but not just any cars—luxury cars. And the legendary Lamborghini was created. History would show that in 2020, over 8,000 Lamborghinis were sold at an average price of $300,000 to $320,000.

Before we get tough on Enzo Ferrari's pride and lack of wisdom, history is littered with people who passed on greatness. Here is just a short list:

- The *Kansas City Star* fired Walt Disney for his lack of imagination and good ideas;
- Blockbuster passed on purchasing Netflix three different times;
- Tom Brady was selected with the 199th pick in the NFL Draft;
- John Travolta turned down the role of Forrest Gump; and
- Chris Daughtry finished fourth in the 2006 *American Idol* contest, losing to Katharine McPhee and Taylor Hicks.

And I could go on and on.

So why do so many smart leaders make such bad decisions? Here are several ideas:

They overestimate their own importance. Their success has made them feel they are the repository of all great ideas. Another thought is they stop learning. After all, why should a super-successful person listen to a moderately successful person? This creates an internal echo chamber, and they no longer listen to outside voices. We hate to admit it but another reason may be appearances. They discount others because of superficial items, such as age, height, weight, ethnicity, sex, attractiveness, and nationality.

There could be another more obvious reason. Let's not overcomplicate this. They simply can't evaluate opportunity. Another reason is they have become addicted to comfort and don't want to deal with inconvenient ideas or realities. After all, no one likes change but a baby, even successful leaders. Therefore, they miss great ideas and make bad decisions. In addition, there is often a financial cost associated with change. There is also often an emotional cost associated with change. You often lose great friends who have been with you for years.

It is the rare leader who has the humility and self-awareness to admit their own ideas are stale and someone might have a better idea. When someone discounts you or your idea, it may not be a reflection of you or your idea at all. It may be a reflection of their inability to evaluate opportunity. There is a difference between sensing opportunity and seizing it. Do any describe you? You don't want to be the leader who passes on the next Lamborghini.

September 14—Stray Cat Falls from Upper Deck

Craig Cromer is an employee of the University of Miami. He and his wife Kimberly are also season-ticket holders of the football team. At each game, he brings an American flag and drapes it over the Section 207 railing where the couple sits. During this past weekend's game, the Cromers noticed a strong sense of urine in the air. Perplexed, they looked up and were shocked to see a cat hanging on for its life from the upper deck of the stadium. The crowd gasped as the cat fell to what was certain to be the loss of one of its nine lives, but the unexpected hero, Craig Cromer, caught the cat using his American flag.

What are the leadership lessons you can take from this harrowing experience?

Average people can still do extraordinary things. In an instant, the Cromers became heroes. So can you. If you feel insignificant, don't believe the lie. God can still do extraordinary things through ordinary people. When opportunity arrives, it's too late to prepare. The Cromers did not come to the game thinking they would be part of a viral moment. But in a moment's notice, they suddenly found themselves involved in saving a cat's life. They had to act immediately.

Use the tools and resources you have available. All the Cromers had at their disposal was an American flag, but that was enough. As a leader, you already have everything you need to be a success as well. Go just a few pages back for more information on this topic. You must constantly stay alert. Problems can creep in from anywhere at any time. Ranchers have a term called "walking the fence" that means they walk their entire property looking for holes in their fences. A hole in the fence could be a place where their valued animals can leave the property or unwanted animals like coyotes can come in kill their livestock.

A stadium security guard, speaking on the condition of anonymity, stated animals often enter the stadium and eat the leftover or discarded food. The cat obviously entered the stadium and made its way to the upper deck. Leaders must always stay alert because bad habits, inefficiencies, competitors, disruptions, and threats to their culture can unknowingly enter their organization or life.

Despite a game going on, everyone became riveted by the drama of a cat potentially falling to its death from the upper deck. However, thanks to the Cromers, the cat survived and a massive celebration broke out. Here's the lesson—Few things bring people together like tragedy and triumph. No one will remember that the University of Miami defeated Appalachian State 25–23. But everyone will remember a cat falling from the upper deck into an American flag.

September 16—Secretariat

On June 9, 1973, over 90,000 horse racing enthusiasts descended on Belmont Park near New York City in hopes of seeing an uber-popular stallion named Secretariat win the Triple Crown. They would not be disappointed. Secretariat sprinted around the one and a half-mile track in two minutes and twenty-four records, winning by an astonishing thirty-one lengths over the next closest competitor. His still record-time has stood for almost fifty years. Photographer Bob Coglianese took the famous picture of jockey Ron Turcotte looking over his shoulder at the remaining horses far behind in the distance.

There is something quite noticeable about this moment from a leadership perspective. Ron Turcotte is looking at what is behind him. Those in attendance were looking at what was behind Secretariat. The announcers were talking about what was behind Secretariat. You know who was not looking behind Secretariat?

Secretariat, that's who.

Secretariat was looking straight ahead. Secretariat was focused on what was before him. Secretariat was prioritizing the task at hand. Secretariat knew the race wasn't over. Secretariat understood there was work yet to be done. Successful leaders approach life and their assignments in the same manner. They are laser-focused on what lies ahead. Leaders are forward-thinking. They are focused on what's next. What is in their windshield is always bigger than their what's in their rearview mirror.

Nothing is worse than spending time with someone whose stories are all from twenty years ago or longer. You are a leader. Your best days should be in the future.

Looking behind can only add value to leaders in two ways:

1. If looking at past failure, it provides data points on what is needed to improve moving forward.
2. If looking at past successes, it should only be used to give you confidence that if you do the right things, success can be achieved again.

Past that, we need to learn from Secretariat's example. Let everyone else look at what is behind. As a leader, you're focused on what's in the future. You're thinking about what's next. There is work left to be done.

September 18–The 1986 New York Mets

The New York Mets won the 1986 World Series in seven legendary games against the Boston Red Sox. Recently, ESPN chronicled the team's journey to success in a four-part installment, *30 for 30* series entitled "Once Upon a Time in Queens." The team reflected the city of New York itself and the debauchery of the mid-'80s. It was a time when high-profile athletes could experience all the gold, glory, girls, violence, and drugs the world had to offer, and many of the Mets did. Their reckless lifestyle did not prevent short-term success. But for all who participated in the excesses of life, their long-term success was dramatically impacted. As I wrote in my book *Timeless: 10 Enduring Practices of Apex Leaders,* you do not need character to get to the top of your profession. But you need character to stay there.

In the mid-'80s, New York City was in a state of crisis. There was racial strife, high crime, and growing economic disparities. But the entire city rallied around this team of larger-than-life personalities who partied hard, cussed like sailors, and would fight you in an instant. The team brought the entire city together. Not matter your lot in life, everyone in New York was a Mets fan.

Shortly after winning the World Series, general manager Frank Cashen elected not to re-sign third baseman Ray Knight and out-fielder Kevin Mitchell. Unknowingly, he dismantled the team's toughness and chemistry. The chemistry the following year was not the same, and neither was the team's performance. You need toughness to succeed in New York. Cashen did not know why the Mets were winning and therefore caused it to lose. A final thought on the famous Game 6 victory. Smart leaders know there is a difference between sensing opportunity and seizing it.

Here is what all had to happen for the Mets to score three runs in bottom of the tenth inning after two outs with no one on base to win the Game 6:

- Boston Red Sox manager John McNamara took out Cy Young pitcher Roger Clemmons earlier in the eighth inning, leading 3–2. The Red Sox would give up a run, taking the game into extra innings.
- Throughout the season, McNamara would take Bill Buckner out late in games for defensive purposes and put in Dave Singleton. He left Bucker in.
- Compassion exceeded good judgment. McNamara left Buckner in because he wanted to allow him to be on the field when the Red Sox won the World Series.
- Gary Carter got a base hit with two outs and one strike off Calvin Schiraldi.
- Kevin Mitchell got a pinch-hit single with two outs off Schiraldi.
- McNamara did not pull Schiraldi after two successive hits.
- Ray Knight got a base hit with two strikes, driving in Carter. Mets are down by one run.

- McNamara pulls Schiraldi and brings in Bob Stanley to pitch.
- Mookie Wilson fouls off countless pitches.
- Stanley throws a wild pitch, allowing Mitchell to score. Game tied.
- Wilson fouls off two more pitches.
- Mookie Wilson hits a slow roller to Buckner, an error is made, and the rest is baseball history.

The Red Sox sensed opportunity and did not seize it. This then created opportunity for the Mets who did.

September 22—The Questions Your Organization Should Be Asking

Does the measurement of 4 feet, 8.5 inches mean anything to you? Trust me, it does more than you know. The Roman Empire ruled the world from 27 BC through AD 476. Their primary mode of transportation and means for patrolling their territory was the two-horse war chariot. The width of the chariot's axles was 4 feet, 8.5 inches or basically two horses side-by-side. As the chariots traveled across the region, their wheels left deep ruts in the ground. This caused significant problems for farmers whose wagons would then get stuck in those ruts. Since their axles were not the same width as the Roman chariots, one of the wagon wheels would often break, trying to get it out of the ground and back on the road. In a classic case of "If you can't beat them, join them," wagons were then redesigned to a width of 4 feet, 8.5 inches. Farmers could now travel freely and without concern throughout the Roman countryside.

Innovation took a while, but eventually it came along with railways used for mining. However, the first mining carts were pulled by horses. As a result, the first railways were built, you guessed it, 4 feet 8.5 inches wide. Welcome to the new Roman two-horse war chariot! Europe eventually decided to put trains on tracks rather than horses. After all, trains were bigger, faster, more efficient, and could carry a heavier load. The trains were bigger, but the tracks stayed the same, remaining 4 feet, 8.5 inches wide.

Surely, the Americans would improve on this concept. Nope! Americans built railroad tracks 4 feet, 8.5 inches wide. Then along came NASA. These people are so innovative they put men on the moon. They would certainly do something different. Not so fast! When NASA began constructing their solid rocket boosters in Utah and transporting them to Florida, they realized the rockets needed to fit on railroad tracks 4 feet, 8.5 inches wide. The rockets are a bit larger, but the reality is NASA constructed the size of some of their rockets partly based upon the size of two horses from the Roman Empire—4 feet, 8.5 inches wide. I bet you will never look at a horse, train, or space shuttle rockets the same way again.

Sometimes it just easier to stick with the status quo. After all, it may have worked for thousands of years! But be warned, don't forget to stop and from time-to-time ask, "Why, exactly, are we doing this?" You may discover there is a better way to do something. A couple of years ago, Los Angeles Rams head coach Sean McVay stopped playing his starters in preseason. Critics lashed out and talked about how his players would be physically and mentally unprepared for the season. The Rams won their first eight games.

A rut is nothing but a grave with the ends kicked out. Is it possible the time has come for your organization to ask some provocative questions about why you are doing the things the way you are?

September 25—The Thing Most Leaders Are Missing

In 2013, a youth indoor soccer tournament was being held in Rockville Centre, New York. During one of the matches, the tournament's organizers discovered they were a referee short. An organizer went to the parents and asked if anyone knew the rules well enough to help out. An unassuming man volunteered to step in. As the match progressed, the man stepped beyond the boundaries of a typical referee. He would periodically stop the game and offer both teams coaching on the importance of proper positioning. In stereotypical fashion, the insufferable parents grew quite frustrated and began to harass the volunteer referee. "Come on! Let them play!" the parents were yelling.

The unassuming referee who just wanted to add value turned out to be Pep Guardiola. At that time, Guardiola had already won two Champions League titles for Barcelona and was one of the most decorated managers and players in the history of global soccer. The kids who were playing that day received instruction from the same man who coached Lionel Messi. But their parents had no idea who was in their midst and were complaining about his pace of play. "Ridiculous! Foolish! Ignorant! Complete lack of awareness! How could they miss Pep Guardioa right before their very own eyes?" you say? Before we get too tough on those parents, let me tell you another story.

Joshua Bell is arguably the world's most-accomplished violinist. He reportedly makes $1,000 per minute while performing on stage. *The Washington Post* had a great idea for an impromptu concert. They decided to have Bell perform in one of the area's busiest locations—the DC Metro corridor. DC Metro averaged more than 1,000 people passing through per hour. Those at the newspaper wanted to know how many of these people would stop and enjoy the performance of this true artist. So how many do you think stopped and listened to Bell? 800 (80%)? 700? 600? How about 30 percent of the people? At least 100 right? Surely a minimum of 10 percent of passersby would stop for just a single minute and enjoy one of the world's greatest artisans. That's $1,000 of value provided for you absolutely free by *The Washington Post*. What a gift and privilege, right?

Would you believe only seven people stopped to hear Joshua Bell? 993 people on average walked past arguably the world's best violinist without even a passing glance. They had no idea who was in their midst. How could they miss what a privilege this was?

The following are four leadership lessons we learn from these stories:

First, individual greatness is easy for leaders to miss. Greatness is inherent in everyone, but it's not easy to spot. You likely already have incredible talent and potential within your organization. It's your job as a leader to discover it in your people and bring it to the surface. Second, few people will ever lead with their résumé. Truly talented people don't brag about their accomplishments. They don't have to. That receptionist in your office has incredible talent and skills if you just stop and ask them what they can do to help the organization. That person in the cubicle may be the most insightful person in your organization, and that unassuming gentlemen who just wants to add value may be one of the best in the world at what he does. And if you didn't notice, that street musician you walk by may just be world class. But you will never know unless you take a moment to ask them about their background and what they can bring to the organization.

Third, how you position people matters. In 1992, Steven Segal starred in the movie *Under Siege*. He played the role of Casey Ryback, a simple cook on a naval battleship. But what we learned about Ryback when domestic terrorists took over the ship, was that he was actually a Navy SEAL, trained in explosives, combat, and weaponry who had been demoted for striking an officer. The ship's crew had no idea who he really was. He had been presented to them as a cook. Guardiola was presented to the parents and players as a volunteer referee. Bell was presented to the passers-by as your everyday street musician. How people are positioned matters.

Finally, we learn the folly of our arrogance. When we arrogantly label people and predetermine the level of value they can bring, we set ourselves up for embarrassment and failure. These truths are pregnant with implications. When we pass by the people at our office, workplace, church, or on the street, are we willing to stop and truly see the value those in our midst can bring? Or, are we going to have to deal with disappointment of missed opportunity?

September 27–Justin Tucker's Record Breaking Sixty-Six-Yard Game-Winning Field Goal

The Baltimore Ravens trailed the Detroit Lions 17–16 with only :03 seconds remaining in the game. With the ball at their own forty-eight-yard line, the Ravens sent out kicker Justin Tucker in a desperate attempt to win the game. With a 90.6 percent success rate, Tucker is widely considered the greatest kicker to have ever played the game. However, he would be attempting a sixty-six-yard field goal. No one had ever done this before. The league record was sixty-four yards, and Tucker was consistently missing from sixty-five yards in practice.

What happened next was historic! Tucker went through his normal progression and kicked the ball with perfect form. As players looked on and the ball sailed majestically through the air, they realized the ball actually had a chance to clear the crossbar. Miraculously, the ball landed on the crossbar and bounced through the goal posts. Pandemonium and an on-field celebration broke out. The Ravens won the game 19-17.

The next day Tucker appeared on *The Dan Patrick Show* to discuss the record-breaking kick. He provided four comments and lessons, which provide a glimpse into what is required to perform at a record-breaking, elite level. Whether you lead a church, business, nonprofit, or athletic organization, if you want to perform at a similar level, read the lessons below.

Elite-level leaders think execution over feelings

Tucker said, "The feelings in those moments don't matter. What matters is executing." What separates average performers from elite performers? It is the ability to execute under pressure. When the pressure is on, locker room speeches and hyping yourself up do not provide lasting results. Execution does.

Also, smart leaders know to do something you've never done before, you're going to have to do things you've never done before. The wonderful website, The33rdTeam.com, reported that Tucker adjusted his mechanics before making the kick. Tucker said, "When you're that far away, you've got to both trust your technique and also sacrifice some of it to just power the ball." What are you willing to sacrifice to achieve things you've never achieved before?

Elite-level leaders think execution over consequences

When performing at a high level, you must trust your preparation and execution and leave the results to themselves. Tucker said, "It's about thinking about the action and not the consequence."

Speaking of consequences, elite-level leaders only celebrate after accomplishment

A leader who doesn't celebrate is a leader not worth following. However, you must know when the proper time to celebrate is.

It's not appropriate to party all the time. Tucker knows celebration should take place only after accomplishment. He said, "When it's all said and done, then you can let your feelings take over and enjoy the moment and your teammates."

Execution. Sacrifice. Proper Thinking. Accomplishment. Celebration. These five things, in that order, will help you potentially see record-breaking results as well.

September 28–Not Knowing What Business You Are Truly In

Ray Croc mistakenly thought he was in the burger business. In the brilliant movie, *The Founder*, Croc was becoming financially insolvent trying to sell hamburgers. He was close to losing his home and going out of business. As a result of an impromptu meeting with Harry Sonneborn, he then discovers he is looking at everything all wrong. Croc was not in the burger business. He was actually in the real estate business. The greatest value Sonneborn brought Croc was properly framing his business.

He said, "You don't seem to realize what business you're in. You're not in the burger business. You're in the real estate business. You don't build an empire off a 1.4 percent cut of a fifteen-cent hamburger. You build it by owning the land on which that burger is cooked." Croc would not be the first or last to not understand what business he was actually in.

In the 1960s and '70s, Polaroid dominated the instant photography market. In the late '90s, the company was the top seller of digital photography. However, their priority was still paper print. Gary DiCamillo, the company's former CEO, told a Yale audience in 2008, "People were betting on hard copy and media that was going to be pick-up-able, visible, seeable, touchable, as a photograph would be." They had the digital photography already in their grasp but were still focused on print photography you could pick up at your local drug store. When paper print photos went the way of the dinosaur, the company was totally shocked. Polaroid made the mistake of thinking they were in the picture business when, in fact, they were in the "creating memories" business.

After purchasing World Championship Wrestling, Ted Turner called World Wrestling Federation owner Vince McMahon. In a paraphrased conversation, he told Vince he was now in "the rasslin' business." Vince responded by saying he was in the entertainment business.

Herb Kelleher is the founder and former CEO of Southwest Airlines. Kelleher had a relentless, almost maniacal, focus on being a "low-fare airline." One day a new marketing employee suggested testing chicken salad instead of peanuts as the snack on its Houston to Las Vegas flights. I can just hear the young, eager rep with fresh eyes saying, "After all, it would be healthier, trendier, newsworthy, and more attractive to young, hip travelers. This would help reach the all-important eighteen to thirty-four demographic." Kelleher responded by asking, "Will adding the entrée help make us a low-fare airline?" Southwest still to this very day serves peanuts on all its flights, especially Houston to Las Vegas. Southwest Airlines is in the low-cost travel business, not the upscale trendy-travel business.

Many churches today have lost their way. They think they are in the social justice business, the entertainment business, the political business, community care business, or TED Talk business. Successful churches who are making an impact are in the disciple-making business.

The NFL Draft is not a talent selection meeting to stock its football franchises with cheap labor. The League knows the Draft is the most highly anticipated and most compelling reality show on television. And it produces it as such. Much like the WWE, the NFL is in the entertainment business.

Many years ago a church consulting company had a spirited internal debate. What type of company were they? Many factions of the organization had their own specific points of view.

One group said they were a ministry. Another said they were a consulting company. Others chimed in saying they were a friend to pastors. There were even comments about being a content-creation company. Finally, the exasperated CEO slammed his fist down on the table and shouted, "We are a *sales* company! Nothing happens until we get the contract!" He knew what business he was in. Do you?

John Maxwell's Law of Priorities says that leaders never confuse activity with accomplishment. Leaders understand you can have movement without progress. Some call this sideways energy. A proper focus prioritizes your efforts and activities. Focus allows you to edit out the non-essentials.

October 5–"The Secret"–Seven Steps to a Winning Culture

In 2007, ESPN columnist Bill Simmons was concerned about getting physically assaulted. In other words, there was a chance he could get beat up like a kid in the schoolyard. Why? A little background: as he describes in his excellent November 5, 2019, *Book of Basketball 2.0 Podcast*, Simmons had been continually hammering away at Isaiah Thomas's ineptitude as the general manager of the New York Knicks. So frustrated by the constant peppering, Thomas went on Stephen A. Smith's radio program and threatened "trouble" if he met Simmons on the street. Well, the day of reckoning had finally arrived. In summer 2008, they ran into each other in Las Vegas. With the help of announcer Gus Johnson playing the role of peacekeeper, Simmons and Thomas actually talked for thirty minutes and developed a certain level of cordialness. What they connected over most was a discussion about the classic Celtics-Pistons rivalry in the 1980s. For those of who may not know, Thomas was the Pistons superstar point guard and Simmons is the biggest Boston sports homer you will ever find.

The conversation went to a completely different level when Simmons brought up "The Secret." What is "The Secret" you ask? The Pistons lost in the '87 and '88 play-offs in heartbreaking fashion to the Celtics and Lakers, respectfully. Sports fans will always remember "Bird steals the ball!" and Thomas's sprained ankle. However, the '89 Pistons finally broke through and won the NBA Championship. During those Finals, Thomas brought up "The Secret" to winning championships to a group of reporters who, at the time, did not know the amount of leadership gold being dropped on them. It went over their heads. But Simmons never forgot the following quotes about "The Secret" and brought it up nineteen years later!

Thomas told the reporters, "It's hard not to be selfish. The art of winning is complicated by statistics, which for us becomes money. But you have to fight that, find a way around it, and I think we have. If we win this, we'll be the first team in history to win it without a single player averaging twenty points. We've got twelve guys who are totally committed to winning. Every night we found a different person to win it for us."

He added, "Lots of times on our team you can't tell who the best player in the game was 'cause everyone did something good. That's what makes us so good. The other team has to think about stopping eight or nine people instead of two or three. It's the only way to win. The only way to win . . . You've also got to create an environment that won't accept losing."

Simmons would ask Thomas nineteen years later what was "The Secret." Thomas smiled and said, "The Secret about basketball is it's not about basketball." What??? In 1988, Adrian Dantley was a NBA All-Star for the Pistons who did not want to sacrifice his personal points for the overall good of the team. He wanted his statistics and the personal benefits which came with them. More money. More notoriety. Prestige. But the Pistons were building a different kind of team, and Dantley's attitude was hurting the culture and the team's ability to win consistently. As a result, Dantley was traded for Thomas's close friend Mark Aguirre. The team's chemistry improved dramatically, and the Pistons won the next two NBA championships.

Pat Riley famously wrote about the challenges championship teams face after success called "The Disease of Me." Dantley embodied this disease, and the Pistons cut him out like a cancer. As Simmons points out, the Pistons ultimately became a dynasty because:

1. They liked each other;
2. They knew and accepted their roles;
3. They sacrificed personal statistics;
4. They valued winning over everything else;
5. Their best player, Isaiah Thomas, sacrificed the most to make everyone else happy;
6. Everyone remained on the same page; and
7. They did the little things winning teams do.

"The Secret about basketball is it's not about basketball."

Could your organization say the same thing?

Whether you lead a church, business, athletic organization, or non-profit, "The Secret" to your winning culture is not in your policies, procedures, and systems. You must have those seven things in place to have long-term success.

October 13—How to Know When a Leader Trusts You

In 1998, a company's executive leadership team was meeting to begin the process of setting up its automatic phone system. This particular project required the writing of multiple scripts and the subsequent implementation of its entire messaging system. Included in this process was the welcome message and then multiple prompts based upon what a customer needed. For example, "To make a payment, press 1. To speak to a customer service representative, press 2. To report a missing or stolen card, press 3," and so on and so on. When the manager asked for a volunteer to head up this project, a young man raised his hand. When doing so, the other leaders looked at each other with raised eyebrows and serious doubt. It was obvious and uncomfortable. Perhaps you've been in a similar meeting.

The manager reluctantly allowed the young man to lead the project but assigned a very skilled leader to work alongside him as back-up. The young man who raised his hand was me. I was *a long* way from becoming Brian Dodd On Leadership! Because of some previous failed initiatives, the other leaders lacked confidence in me. They did not trust me, particularly my attention to detail and follow-through skills. Recently, I thought about that humbling experience twenty-five years ago.

This past Sunday, the Los Angeles Chargers defeated the Cleveland Browns 47–42. It was a high-scoring, thrilling game. Rather than choosing to punt, on four different occasions each team went for it on fourth-down. Even though these were high-risk decisions, the Chargers converted each of their four opportunities into first downs. Why was head coach Brandon Staley so aggressive? One reason may be the Browns were scoring so often he had to go for it. But the main reason is because of Staley's confidence in the person executing the fourth-down plays—second-year superstar quarterback Justin Herbert.

Tom Brady once said, "To me what separates really good players from great players—they execute well under pressure. The biggest game. The biggest stage. That's what playing quarterback is all about." And Justin Herbert knows how to play quarterback. He finished the game completing 26 or 43 passes for 398 yards and 4 touchdowns.

Conversely, with 2:55 left in the game and the Browns facing a third-down and nine yards to go for a first down, the team inexplicably ran the ball, instead of having quarterback Baker Mayfield try to complete a pass. The play was unsuccessful, and the team was forced to punt. It would appear the team's head coach Kevin Stefanski does not have nearly the confidence in his quarterback as the Chargers do in Herbert. If this is truly the case, I can relate to Mayfield. I've been there.

So how do you know when a leader trusts you? The leader trusts you when they assign you important and complex tasks in high-pressure situations.

The Chargers put the ball in Herbert's hands on four fourth-down plays, and he executed each time. The Browns put the ball in the running back's hands with less than three minutes to go. The Chargers and head coach Brandon Staley trusted Herbert and justifiably so? Does your organization have an equal amount of trust in you?

October 16—How Dabo Swinney Gets Big Financial Gifts From Wealthy People

Leon J. Hendrix Jr. was the student body president for Clemson University in 1963. He later attended its graduate school, and each of his four children attended the university as well. Hendrix went on to spend ten years heading up the gun manufacturer Remington Arms. And Hendrix loved Clemson's football team, so much so he put his money where his mouth was. Hendrix had recently donated several hundred thousand dollars to aid in the construction of the team's new locker room facility. He and his wife Pam felt this was more than enough of an investment for them to make and they were done.

On October 29, 2012, Terry Don Phillips was named Clemson's athletic director. He soon asked head football coach Dabo Swinney what would be needed to consistently challenge for national championships. Swinney already had the answer ready. He then sketched out a state-of-the-art football facility. Proverbs 29:18 (KJV) says, "Where there is no vision, people perish." John Maxwell adds, "Where there are no resources, the vision perishes." Phillips immediately knew significant dollars would be needed for Swinney's vision to not perish but become reality.

Coach Swinney and previous AD Dan Radakovich had put together the funding plan for the new facility. It included the school's high-capacity supporters needing to give individual donations of $2.5 million. This was a significant issue. No one in the school's history had ever given an athletic donation of such size. The key to the plan was getting Hendrix on board. If he would be willing to participate at that level, Radakovich and Swinney knew other financial leaders would join in and follow suit. In June of 2012, Coach Swinney traveled to the Hendrix home on Kiawah Island, located just south of Charleston, South Carolina. The two sat down on the porch overlooking the Atlantic Ocean when Swinney began casting vision for a 140,000-square-foot complex, featuring amenities, such as a bowling alley, movie theater, volleyball courts, laser tag, barber shop, and much, much more. The total cost would be $55 million and require $35.5 million in contributions.

Coach Swinney went on explain the important role elite facilities play in the arms race of college football recruitment of elite talent. And this would give Clemson a significant advantage. Everything would be designed with the athlete in mind. During the conversation Swinney asked Hendrix if he saw Clemson win their only national title in 1981. Hendrix emphatically said he did. Then Swinney asked the right question: "Do you ever want to win another one?" This was the perfect question. He tapped into Hendrix's passion.

Lars Anderson in his book *Dabo's World: The Life and Career of Coach Swinney and the Rise of Clemson Football* then records the following exchange:

"'Well,' Dabo said, jabbing himself in the chest his forefinger, "I'm your best hope." Dabo then paused, locked his eyes on Hendrix, and said, "And you're my best hope." Not only did Hendrix give the program $2.5 million, his wife Pam wondered if they gave enough.

The groundbreaking ceremony for the team's new complex took place in November 2015. Coach Swinney addressed those in attendance, "When I got this job, everybody talked about the good old days. Everybody walks around like the best is behind us. I'm telling you, the best is yet to come. This is the good old days. This is the best of times. And what this facility does, what this facility means when we stick a shovel in the ground, what we're saying is the best is yet to come."

Coach Swinney was right. Since the groundbreaking the team has won two more national championships.

October 23–The One Thing the Greatest Leaders Do (Which Others Don't) to Become Successful

In early 1994, former San Francisco 49ers head coach Bill Walsh received a phone call from an old friend and former player, but it wasn't just any player. Quarterback Joe Montana was reaching out with a surprising request. Montana was asking Coach Walsh to review his mechanics and footwork. Montana simply felt they were not as precise as they should be. Something felt off. What was surprising about this request was Montana's professional status. You see, by this time Montana was a fifteen-year veteran, two-time National Football League Most Valuable Player, four-time Super Bowl champion, and his place in the Hall of Fame was already secure. Many were already viewing him as the greatest quarterback of all-time.

And yet, he was focused on among other things— footwork. Why would the greatest quarterback to ever play the game at that point spend so much time on fundamentals? Because Montana knew the reason he was the greatest quarterback of all-time at that point was he spent so much time on his fundamentals. Joe Montana and all of the greatest leaders know their success is directly tied to their mastery of fundamentals. Making a *big* deal of little things is often the difference between success and failure. The greatest leaders know how you do anything is how you do everything. And they never get bored working on them.

The reason so many leaders bypass the fundamentals in their training and daily work is they simply hate the grind. The grind is the day-in, day-out unattractive work that receives no applause or fanfare. It is the lonely work done in secret. It's boring. It's hard to see the results. However, it is grinding through the lonely, boring work, which ultimately leads to public applause.

Whatever work you are involved in, whether it be in ministry, business, athletics, or nonprofit, there are elements of your job you do not enjoy. It's boring. There's no applause. However, it is the mastery of these little things, which will allow you to reach your full potential as a leader. So I have a challenge for you.

Are you ready to be like Joe Montana and other great leaders and embrace the grind and press through these challenges? The greatest leaders have done so, and it is what has made them successful.

October 25—What One of His Campus Pastors Learned from Andy Stanley

For thirteen years, Gavin Adams was the lead and campus pastor for Woodstock (Georgia) City Church. Located just north of Atlanta, this church was a campus of North Point Ministries led by Andy Stanley. During Gavin's tenure, the church grew to an active database of 38,000 with an average weekly attendance of 8,000. Recently, Gavin felt God was moving him from Woodstock City to begin coaching marketplace and ministry leaders full-time. Today, Gavin helps leaders make things better and make better things. In an interview on *The Pursuit of Service Podcast* which I co-host with Jeff Wright, we had the privilege of interviewing Gavin about topics, such as healthy cultures, vision alignment, and behaviors which lead to success. One of the first topics we discussed was what he learned during his time working with and for Andy. We discussed five areas.

First, was a discussion on family. As Gavin pointed out, Andy has communicated often on the subject of balancing family and ministry. He would meet very early to help people but would be home by 4:30 p.m. Following Andy's lead, Gavin was often the first person in the office but was home in the late afternoon to serve his family. Quoting Andy, Gavin said, "At some point someone else is going to have my job . . . But I don't want anyone else to be a husband to my wife or father to my kids. That's the one job I never want anyone else to have. So that's my number one priority."

Next, we discussed the subject of humility. Few Christian leaders in church history have the résumé of Andy Stanley. He could easily have a "I have this figured out"–type of attitude. But one of the things that makes Andy so successful is he is a continual learner, and one of the groups of people he learns the most from is his staff. Gavin said, "I worked for Andy, directly with Andy. But when you work for Andy, you work with Andy. I was impressed over my eleven years how frequently he wanted to know my opinion, how he valued my perspective, how he wanted to learn because we have very different personalities. He valued diversity and inclusion of all kinds, including personality diversion and inclusion."

Andy was also a master delegator. You simply cannot run a ministry as vast as North Point Ministries without delegating responsibilities. Gavin pointed out, "That's what great leaders do. He delegated a lot to guys like me. He trusted people like me." One of the areas Andy trusted Gavin in was preaching and communicating. Gavin fondly remembered, "Andy only actually reviewed one sermon outline before I preached it. From that point forward, he allowed me to do whatever God laid on my heart and trusted me in the process."

We also discussed the subject of continual improvement. Andy has previously taught that the greatest enemy of future success is current success. Regarding Andy evaluating his sermons, Gavin said, "Andy helped critique it on the back-end to make it better for the next time but wasn't going to get too involved upfront because he wanted me to learn through the experience of wrestling with all the stuff." I had to ask a follow-up question regarding what it was like to have one of the world's greatest communicators evaluate his preaching. Gavin admitted it could be intimidating and could reveal all your insecurities. However, he counted it as a great privilege. Gavin said, "I just want to be a learner . . . Every version of critique is helpful, even if it's hurtful personally . . . When you can allow it to be about growth and getting better for the next time, sitting with a guy like Andy, it is a doctorate in communication . . . I can't metric how much better of a communicator I am just through osmosis and watching and learning over time with a guy like that."

And finally, we discussed decision-making. Because of their personalities, Gavin and Andy approach decision-making completely differently. Gavin said, "Andy is not a quick decision-maker . . . Andy's a little bit more of a perfectionist . . . Andy's pacing in big decisions was helpful for me to learn . . . By slowing down it gives us the ability to process information better, to bring more people into the conversation, allow that to marinate, and allow all those things collectively to lead to the best decision in the end. He does a good, good job of that."

October 27–Two Things You Must Have to Lead When You're Not in Charge

In 1994, a public utility went through deregulation. As part of this process, thirteen local offices were consolidated into a single call center. As with any downsizing initiative, many employees took early retirement. Sadly, many more were forced to take a severance package. However, approximately one hundred employees were retained.

One of the teams formed in this call center was an elite group of individuals, hand-picked from each of the local offices. These were the best of the best. They would be in charge of multiple special projects. Recovering lost revenue due to meter failure was one of the most high-profile. The leader of the group setup a special training session within the first few weeks and selected two people she felt comfortable with to equip the others. However, one young man felt he was as equally skilled as the two who were selected. He was, after all, part of the elite group and did not lack for confidence. During the training, he acted disinterested and many times attempted to take over the meeting. At the end of the meeting, he announced he was conducting his own training session later in the day and invited anyone who wished to attend.

When the time for his unplanned, impromptu training session was to take place, no one showed up. Absolutely no one. He was not in charge. The leader of the department was. He was not in charge of training for this initiative. Two others were. But when he raised his hand, proactively took the mantle of leadership and said "Follow me," no one did. Why? After being embarrassed and humbled, he learned some important lessons.

First, the team had only been together a few weeks. Relationships and trust had not had time to form. If you are going to lead when you're not in charge, there must be some relational equity. Trust needs to be built through a track record of success. People must have confidence you can deliver. Second, hubris. This young man was extremely arrogant. He thought he was better than anyone else on that elite team. Interestingly, he may have been right. But because he had not built trust among his peers, he was not going to be given the opportunity to demonstrate his skills and capabilities. Rather than hubris, he needed humility.

Leaders, if you are new to an organization and want to make a leadership impact, start by building relationships. Develop trust and build chemistry with your new teammates. Second, be humble. Have the posture of a learner. There are many talented people around you to learn from. Have the humility to do so.

These are two lessons about leading when you're not in charge that my friend learned the hard way. Maybe now you don't have to.

November 3—The Story of Two Great Leaders Who Created a Five-Step Strategy for Giving Encouragement

Coach Keith Madison served as head baseball coach at the University of Kentucky for twenty-five years (1979–2003). During his tenure he amassed 737 wins and has been inducted into three Halls of Fame: Kentucky High School Baseball Hall of Fame, University of Kentucky Hall of Fame, and the American Baseball Coaches Association Hall of Fame. In 2013, Keith was honored with the Lefty Gomez Award. Since then, he has been working with SCORE International. Coach Madison can now combine two of the passions in his life: his faith and baseball. He reaches hundreds of college and high school baseball coaches and friends through his biweekly devotions and has spoken to thousands of coaches and players in sixteen states and the Dominican Republic. Coach Madison is a godly man and great leader.

Kevin Burrell is the area scouting supervisor with the Chicago White Sox. He has worked in pro baseball as both a player and MLB scout for the past forty years. Kevin was originally selected in the first round of the 1981 free-agent amateur draft (twenty-fifth overall) and played ten years of professional baseball with four different organizations. He reached as high as Triple-A before finishing his playing career in 1992. Those who know Kevin describe him as a pastor disguised as a scout.

Each week, I have the privilege of joining approximately eighty professional and amateur baseball coaches and scouts for an online Bible study. This time together is put on by Mike Linch, the incomparable senior pastor of NorthStar Church in Kennesaw, Georgia. This is my favorite forty-five minutes of the week. Recently, we were studying the life of Barnabas and what made him such a great encourager. A question was asked of Coach Madison and Kevin about how to best encourage people. As they spoke, I knew these two men were dispensing leadership gold. I took copious notes of everything they said and then constructed the following five-step plan for encouragement from their thoughts:

1. **Be Intentional**—We do not default into encouragement. Coach Madison, like all of us, wishes he would have done more of this when he was younger. Being an encourager is a decision. Kevin coached us up by saying it takes focus and discipline.

2. **Develop a Plan**—A failure to plan is a plan to fail. As leaders, we must develop a system of encouragement we practice regularly. Put it on your calendar if you have to.

3. **Meet One-on-One with People**—This was the process recommended by Coach Madison. An encouraging message to the entire team is not enough. For maximum impact, a one-on-one heartfelt conversation from you as the leader is necessary.

4. **Be Specific and Give Next Steps**—Go to those on your team and be specific about the areas you want to encourage them in. This encouragement could be for improvement, motivation, or confirmation, but you must be specific.

5. **Evaluate**—These are coaches and scouts after all. They look at the scoreboard. Did their encouragement have the desired results they were looking for? The measurement of success is generally transformation (Did life change take place?), not transaction (I checked off the box that I encouraged someone today).

As Truett Cathy said, someone you know needs encouraging today. If you don't know the best way to do so, use this five-step plan. You will be glad you did—and more importantly, so will they.

November 6–Can One Person Change an Organization's Culture?

Can one person change an organization's culture? More importantly, can you personally change your organization's culture? It is a rarity, but in certain situations, I think it is absolutely possible.

The Tampa Bay Buccaneers finished the 2019 NFL season with a 7–9 record. The Bucs were quite talented, but inconsistency at the quarterback position severely limited the team's potential. The team's general manager Jason Licht and head coach Bruce Arians felt the solution to their problem was a person, specifically legendary quarterback Tom Brady. On March 20, 2020, the team signed Brady to a two-year contract.

On that day, the culture throughout the entire organization changed. The results were obvious. But no one could really explain how Brady did it—until now. Upon signing his contract, Tom began to promptly change the team's culture. In an unusual move, he got the cell numbers for *all* the players and reached out to each one individually. He then immediately went to work and began organizing team workouts with the running backs and wide receivers. These were such must-attend events that lineman and defensive players began attending as well, many coming in from out of town. As the team began working together, no one wanted to disappoint Tom. Offensive lineman would apologize for missing blocks, receivers would apologize for not catching passes, and vowed to do better.

Tom also attracted skilled players like Rob Gronkowski, Leonard Fournette, and Antonio Brown throughout the course of the year. But ultimately, Tom just wants to be one of the guys. His humility helped changed the team's culture. But that wasn't all, throughout the season and regardless of the circumstance, Tom never lost his cool. He never showed panic or confusion. Tom was consistent in his demeanor and approach. He brought a sense of calm to the entire team.

Most importantly, Tom's mere presence expanded the frontiers of what everyone thought was possible. They could now dream about all possibilities, including winning the Super Bowl. It cannot be overstated how much confidence Brady gave to this very talented team. They knew they could win any game or come back from any deficit as long as he was their quarterback. Because if Tom Brady is on your team, you always have hope.

You also learn the value of preparation. Let's start with the obvious: young players watched how he took care of his body. They also watched how he used his mind. Players were sent home iPads to study. Their time online was tracked by the coaches. Tom studied more than anyone on the team. Finally, they watched him in team meetings. Tom always sat in the front row and took notes like a rookie who was trying to impress the coach and make the team.

During practice Tom was very demanding of everyone. He was unforgiving with poor habits or execution. Everything had to be done perfectly or they would do it again. Tom focused relentlessly on fundamentals and continually sought feedback on items, such as his release points and footwork. Coaches and teammates felt he was the most detailed quarterback they had ever seen. Even at his age and with six Super Bowl championships, he still wanted to be coached and get better.

Tom also legitimized the coaches and staff. With his pedigree, if he bought in and performed every drill, everyone else was without excuse. Tom was the greatest pupil on the team. Everything was about hard work. Tom was always the first one to arrive in the building. He also had great self-awareness and was acutely aware of his physical shortcomings. As a result, he could be very efficient and proficient with his actions.

Tom was always hyper-focused on football. As a result, Tom basically operated as a player-coach and gave precise feedback to the players on what they needed to improve on. He was deeply committed to his teammates' success and helping them improve, and that's all players want. When Tom spoke, everyone listened. His words to his teammates were always firm and final. Because the feedback was coming from Tom Brady, his words meant something. Tom also modeled servant-leadership by continually making sacrifices, both physically and financially, so the team can be better.

Because of everything mentioned above, he led by example, and his habits rubbed off on everyone. What ultimately legitimizes a leader and an organization's culture is results. On a personal level, the forty-four-year-old Brady finished the season with forty touchdown passes and 4,633 yards, both third in the league. But the greatest sign of the culture Brady helped create was on February 7, 2021, when the Tampa Bay Buccaneers defeated the Kansas City Chiefs 31–9 in Super Bowl LV. Tom Brady helped create a championship culture. You could possibly do so as well if you his example.

November 8–Foo Fighters Lead Singer Dave Grohl's Remarkable Interaction with a Special-Needs Fan

Recently, Foo Fighters lead singer Dave Grohl performed an impromptu and extraordinary act of kindness. During a sold-out concert, Growl noticed mid-song a special needs fan having trouble locating a seat. What happened next no one in attendance will ever forget. Grohl stopped singing and immediately worked with those seated in his section to help find the fan a seat.

There are several leadership lessons we can learn from this extraordinary act. As John Maxwell teaches, leader see more than others see. They see before others see. And they see farther than others see. Those on a public stage see more of what is happening in the audience than others. Grohl used his elevated status (both physically on an elevated stage and positionally as the lead singer) to notice the needs of others he was serving.

Grohl then had the right focus. Successful leaders prioritize people over projects, processes, and yes, even profits. I have the privilege of knowing many stage artists. Most are understandably focused on the task at hand. Are the musicians hitting their notes? Are the singers on pitch? Does everyone know their lines? Are my in-ears and monitors properly working? Is the lighting team and other technicians competent? Are the band members and musicians high, sober, or hung over? You get the drift.

Elite performers who are masters of their craft have a different focus. Rather, their focus is on the audience and what their needs are. Is the audience engaged or bored? Are they leaning in or have their arms crossed? What are they responding to? Is there a connection taking place? They then process all this information and adjust their messaging and performance accordingly. Regardless of your profession, you must also have the right focus and prioritize people over projects, processes, and profits.

Being a master of your craft also comes with the added bonus of margin. Having elite talent and expertise affords you the privilege of not having to worry so much about the technical aspects of your job. You have already mastered those. As Nick Saban says, you practiced the fundamentals so much you cannot get them wrong. This frees up your mind to focus on adjustments.

Let me explain. Think of the relationship between expertise and adjustments as 90/10. If you have to spend 90 percent of your time focused on the technical aspects of your job, you then only have 10 percent margin to focus on adjustments like the changing needs of your audience. However, if you know your craft so well you only have to focus 10 percent on the technical aspects, you then have the margin to focus 90 percent of your efforts on adjusting to your audience.

This is why Dave Grohl could stop mid-song and help out a fan in need. He is a master of his craft. His elite talent freed his mind up enough to do so. It cannot be overstated the remarkable level of skill that was required for this act to take place. Grohl also teaches us that leaders must have a radical and immediate response to the needs of others. If you have information, you are responsible for it and must address the issue. Once Grohl noticed the special needs fan struggling with finding a seat, he immediately made sure proper accommodations took place. He took responsibility for the situation as any great leader would.

There are many things a leader can do to reduce their influence. Unhealthy pride. Selfishness. Lack of trust. Poor performance. This is just to name a few. However, two things which always increase influence are generosity and compassion. Grohl was already performing in front of an adoring crowd but what he did that night endeared him with those in attendance forever.

Let's don't make this too complicated. What makes something "remarkable" is people are willing to make a remark about it. In complete transparency, I cannot name you one Foo Fighters song. I know I'm living in a bubble, but I had never heard the name Dave Grohl before watching the video of this exchange. I would also be willing to bet I completely disagree with the band's lifestyle, lyrics, and language. We probably have very little in common. All that being said, the compassion he showed to this special needs fan and what all that had to be in place from a talent perspective for him to do so, is remarkable. So I remarked about it. So should you.

Bonus—After originally writing about this, I had some readers of my site provide additional content I want to pass along. Some risks are worth taking. Grohl ran the risk of alienating the crowd by interrupting the concert by stopping his song and helping someone with a need. In our entitled society, hard-working people paid a lot of money to attend and could have just rolled their eyes. Selfishness is one of the default modes of being human. However, Grohl was letting everyone know that there was somebody there more important than himself and the audience, and they needed help. Therefore, he took a brief moment to show some kindness. Also, it did not take a lot of time and effort to show a little kindness and find someone a seat. But Grohl reminded us that anyone can make a big difference by doing a small act.

What *small* act of kindness can you do today to make a *big* difference in someone else's life?

November 9—You Can't Lead Anyone Unless You First Do This

One of the most famous stories about Mahatma Ghandi concerns a mother who approached him with an unusual request. Wanting to address her daughter's eating habits, she asked, "Would you tell my little girl to stop eating so much candy? She's consuming far too much sugar." As a diabetic, I can appreciate her request. If I were Ghandi, I probably would have responded with some gentle advice for the girl or asked her father to handle it. Another option would be to give the mother some tips she could use. But Ghandi took a different approach.

It is said that after a brief time of contemplation, he told the concerned mother to "come back in two weeks." It was a confusing response, and I'm sure the mother walked away disappointed and perplexed. But undaunted, she returned in two weeks and made the same request. This time Ghandi did advise the young girl to stop eating so much sugar. Now further perplexed, the mother asked Ghandi what was different this time than two weeks prior.

Ghandi said, "Because two weeks ago, I ate too much sugar."

Ghandi knew he had no credibility to make the request of the young girl because he struggled with the same issue. This is wonderful story illustrates several fundamental leadership principles:

- Leaders must lead by example;
- Leaders go first;
- Leadership is a picture of the desired destination at which others should wish to arrive;
- Authenticity requires you walk the walk before you talk the talk; and
- Leaders should never ask anyone to do anything they are unwilling to first do themselves.

What Ghandi also teaches us is you can't lead anyone unless you can first lead yourself. Self-leadership gives you the credibility required to lead others. It gives you the "street cred" needed to ask people to follow you. Experienced leaders know the hardest person to lead is yourself. What self-leadership issues are you currently dealing with which may be hurting your credibility to lead others?

November 11–Three Smart Leaders on What Churches with Growing Onsite Weekend Attendance in 2021 Are Doing

It is common knowledge churches are running an average of 40–50 percent of their pre-COVID attendance this year. But this is not always the case. Many churches are currently thriving! But what is causing these congregations to run against the norm and reach new converts for Christ? I recently had a number of interesting discussions with three top church consultants regarding how pastors and church leaders should view church growth and weekend onsite attendance in 2021.

I talked about Gavin Adams earlier. He is a strategic organizational consultant and leadership partner focused on supporting leaders from innovation through implementation. Before launching Transformation Solutions, Gavin spent fifteen years in ministry leadership, most recently serving as the lead pastor at Woodstock City Church, a campus location of North Point Ministries that had 37,000 active participants and sixty-five staff. Prior to ministry, Gavin spent over a decade in the marketplace, working as a business strategy and marketing consultant. Gavin mentioned to me and co-host Jeff Wright on our *Pursuit of Service Podcast* that churches who are more focused on trying to reach new people rather than getting former attendees back are the ones who are currently prevailing. Your focus should be more outward than backward.

Shawn Lovejoy is founder and CEO of Courage to Lead. His heart beats for coaching leaders and helping them conquer whatever's keeping them up at night. Shawn has been a successful real estate developer, church planter, megachurch pastor, and now CEO of a fast-growing coaching and consulting organization. He specializes in leadership, personal growth, organizational health, and helping leaders create momentum.

Shawn gave me a brilliant numerical equation, 100–40–100. Allow me to explain. Let's say your pre-COVID onsite weekend attendance was 400. After the shutdown concluded, 40 percent returned, and your new weekend average onsite attendance is 160. The first "100" represents 100 percent of your pre-COVID average onsite weekend attendance of 400. The "40" is the 40 percent current average number of people who have returned to onsite attendance after the shutdown. The second "100" is a very important number. This "100" represents 100 percent of your new average weekend attendance of 160 that is showing up. Pastors who evaluate the current reality and quit saying, "We're about 40 percent of what we used to be" and understand their attendance is now 160 are the ones who are beginning to grow again. They say, "This is who we are, and we are going to grow from here."

Jeff Shortridge is a senior consultant for INJOY Stewardship Solutions and author of the wonderful book, *God Honors Movement*, so he is an expert on this topic. He helps churches fully-fund their missions and visions. I recently asked him what is a common thread of churches who are seeing growth and supernatural results. Jeff mentioned the churches who were impacted by COVID but unfazed by COVID are the ones which are now seeing growth and forward movement. Churches were obviously impacted. Many people within the church contracted the virus, and some tragically passed away. Without question COVID impacted churches.

But growing churches remained unfazed regarding their mission and vision. They remained steadfast in focusing on discipleship and evangelism, and now that we are cautiously on "the back end," these churches are seeing the fruits of remaining diligent. They never lost sight of what God wanted them to do. The healthy way for churches to think of their weekend attendance is that they are a new church plant in an existing location with an existing core group of people.

As Shawn noted, if you could plant a church today in a potentially debt-free facility, with a core group of 160 passionate people with a first-year income of $500,000, would you take it? The answer is *absolutely*! Focus on reaching new people more than getting old people back. Forty percent is your new 100 percent. You can be both impacted and unfazed by COVID as a new church plant in an existing location with an existing core group of people. Churches who evaluate reality in this manner and are focused on discipleship and reaching their unchurched friends are still seeing supernatural results in 2021 and beyond.

November 13—Forty Things Average People Don't Do

Tim Elmore asks a great question in his wonderful new book *The Eight Paradoxes of Great Leadership: Embracing the Conflicting Demands of Today's Workplace*, "How long does it take for an average person to earn a black belt in karate?" The answer is interesting. Tim points out that average people don't earn black belts.

Webster defines average as "*a number expressing the central or typical value in a set of data, in particular the mode, median, or (most commonly) the mean, which is calculated by dividing the sum of the values in the set by their number.*"

We have all heard the phrase "they reduced to the mean." This is often used when a team or individual has initial results far above what was expected. Then over time, they performed at the previously expected level. They reduced to the mean or "came back to the pack." The fact is most people and teams are average. A handful are above average and only a select few become elite. However, most are average. But just so you know, the following are forty things average people don't do:

1. Average people don't live extraordinary lives. They live ordinary lives.
2. Average people don't have good habits. Everything is random and happens completely by chance.
3. Average people don't have above average or elite people around them. You are the average of the five people closest to you.
4. Average people don't rise early. They sleep late.
5. Average people don't arrive early. They're always tardy.
6. Average people don't lose weight. They gain weight.
7. Average people don't have a healthy lifestyle. They have an unhealthy lifestyle.
8. Average people don't run marathons. They spend a lot of time on the couch.
9. Average people don't spend hours in prayer and bible study. They don't have an intimate relationship with God.
10. Average people don't serve others. They serve themselves.
11. Average people don't give generously. They are greedy.
12. Average people don't save money. They are in debt.
13. Average people don't write books or even read them. They watch television instead.
14. Average people don't listen to sound advice. They are arrogant and think they know it all.
15. Average people don't become Eagle Scouts. They watch others achieve that goal.

16. Average people don't graduate college early. The average college student takes six years to finish.
17. Average people don't stay married. They get divorced.
18. Average people don't like hard conversations. They are passive-aggressive.
19. Average people don't show kindness. They are angry and confrontational.
20. Average people don't forgive others. They hold grudges.
21. Average people don't go the extra mile. They do the bare minimum.
22. Average people don't make that one extra sales call or do one more rep. They pack up fifteen minutes before it's time to go.
23. Average people don't continually learn. They think they're good enough already.
24. Average people don't like hard work, being stretched, or pushed out of their comfort zone. They are lazy and like the status quo.
25. Average people don't like high expectations. They want their bar set very, very low.
26. Average people don't sacrifice. They are gluttonous.
27. Average people don't appreciate delayed gratification. They want it and want it now.
28. Average people don't welcome accountability. They don't want anyone telling them to improve.
29. Average people don't feel old. They feel young.
30. Average people don't take enough risks. Ironically, not taking risks is the biggest risk of all.
31. Average people don't respect their elders. Or anyone else for that matter.
32. Average people don't focus on the future and what's next. They talk about the good 'ole days.
33. Average people don't talk about fresh ideas. They gossip about people.

34. Average people don't restrain their language, thoughts, behaviors, or words. They are unfiltered, reckless, and destructive.
35. Average people don't think God could do anything extraordinary in their lives today. In fact, they don't think about God at all.
36. Average people don't improve the lives of the people around them. They make them worse.
37. Average people don't promote others. They self-promote.
38. Average people don't get excited about Mondays, only the weekends.
39. Average people don't leave an extraordinary legacy. Many are forgotten by history.
40. Average people don't learn from their mistakes. They commit the same ones over and over again.
41. ***Bonus*** Average people don't finish well. They quit or get disqualified.
42. ***Second Bonus*** Average people don't read leadership books or websites. Only elite people do these things.

November 16–The Most Long-Lasting and Impactful Thing a Leader Can Do

In March of this year, Noah Reeb was a ten-year-old boy fighting brain cancer. After going through two surgeries in a three-week span, Noah and his parents, James and Jacque, were facing desperate times. Hope was in short supply. A miracle was needed. But their fortunes were about to change. Inspiration and encouragement were on the way in the form of a legendary quarterback.

Tom Brady, the GOAT himself and quarterback of the Tampa Bay Buccaneers, unexpectedly sent Reeb a video message, encouraging him to keep fighting. Brady's video provided the fuel Noah needed to not give up. Noah's father James told ESPN's Jeff Darlington, "It (the video) changed his whole approach to cancer."

As Noah's condition improved, James told his son that when he got better they were going to see Tom play in person. That day arrived on Sunday, October 24 when the Buccaneers hosted the Chicago Bears at Raymond James Stadium. Noah and his family had seats on the third row. In an effort to get Tom's attention, Noah brought a sign which read, "Tom Brady Helped Me Beat Brain Cancer." The now-cancer free Noah and his hero Brady were then able to connect at the game's conclusion. Just as Brady surprised Noah with a video message in March, Noah surprised Brady with an in-person visit in October. Their heartwarming story was captured on an *Inside the NFL* feature.

Tom was asked about this moment on his *Let's Go* podcast. His answer reveals the most long-lasting and impactful thing a leader can do. He said, "Caring is what's cool. Caring is what's great leadership. Caring is what the right thing to do is, and when you stop caring about people, it becomes very dysfunctional. We've got to care more about the people who aren't cared for. We've got to care about the people who don't have the opportunities and going through the tough times."

There are many things leaders prioritize which are temporal—monthly earnings, seasonal results, wins and losses, positions and titles, income, and so forth. But leaders should always remember the words of Maya Angelou, "I've learned that people will forget what you said, people will forget what you did, but people will never forget how you made them feel." Noah Reeb and his parents, James and Jacque, would agree.

The most long-lasting and impactful thing you can do as a leader is care for your family, care for your team, care for your customers, care for your community, and care for those without hope. When you do so, people will never forget that you made them feel cared for. Your impact on their life will be long-lasting. It is true what Tom said, caring is cool. Caring is great leadership.

November 17–The Number One Thing Leaders Must Do When Faced with Unexpected Crises or Challenging Times

Located in the Great Smokey Mountains National Park and just minutes away from Pigeon Forge and Dollywood, Gatlinburg, Tennessee, is known for its beautiful views, wedding chapels, countless craft stores, and great pancakes. It is one of the most popular tourist destinations in America. Gatlinburg is also known as a place you can see black bears in the wild. Recently, the town has seen a surge in the number of bears leaving the forests to search for food on the downtown strip. This has resulted in multiple up-close and potentially dangerous personal encounters. While black bears look quite cute and cuddly, people must remember these are wild animals.

Two weeks ago, my wife and I spent a few days in Gatlinburg, just relaxing and getting refreshed after a busy year. To take advantage of a lovely, crisp forty-degree morning, we decided to take a stroll around our hotel's parking lot and look at the beautiful fall leaves. On the back of the property, we stopped for my wife to take pictures of the scenery. Suddenly, I noticed to my left a black bear coming over the ridge approximately ten feet from us. Following the bear were three cubs. This was obviously a mama bear who would no doubt intensely protect her baby bears.

I calmly said to my wife in a soft voice, "Honey, I need you to stay calm and slowly follow me." She turned and noticed the four bears just a few feet away. Placing her behind me we began to back away slowly. I was prepared to act crazy, start waving my arms and screaming loudly, or fight to the death so my wife could escape—whatever was required. Everything turned out fine, and the bears just walked away like we were not there. But let's return for a moment to what I said to my wife during a potentially dangerous encounter, "Honey, I need you to stay calm and slowly follow me."

When crises or challenging times come without warning, leaders must remain calm and then communicate this sense of calm to their teams. This helps others feel secure and remain calm as well. For the leader, remaining calm allows you to think clearly and develop quality strategies. These strategies, once implemented, result in the solutions needed to help you and your team navigate through the crisis.

Here's the flow: Calmness——-> Clear Thinking——-> Quality Strategies——-> Solutions

In a worst-case scenario, the leader must be willing to pay whatever price is needed to protect their team. People are a picture of the leader. Your team will always follow your lead. If you remain calm, they will remain calm. There is a scene in the movie *The American President* where Michael J. Fox tells the president, played by Michael Douglas, and his staff that it is important for everyone to *act* calm. Douglas responds by saying, "I think it's important that everyone *be* calm."

Leaders, be calm, especially if you are walking the streets of Gatlinburg.

November 20–A Leader's Greatest Strength

On Sunday, October 11, 2020, Dallas Cowboys quarterback Dak Prescott dropped back to pass and surveyed the New York Giants' defense. Finding no one open, he then scrambled out of the pocket and began running downfield. Giants cornerback Logan Ryan then executed what appeared to be a routine tackle of Prescott. But something very non-routine happened as Prescott was dragged to the ground. Prescott's leg bent awkwardly;, and he suffered a compound fracture and dislocation of his ankle. His season was over, and his future, both as a potential free agent Cowboy and NFL player, were suddenly in serious question.

But this was not the worst thing to happen to Prescott in 2020. Six months earlier, on April 22, Dak's brother Jace unexpectedly died as a result of suicide. Dak, himself, was no stranger to mental illness as he had struggled with it as well. How does someone possibly recover from mental illness, an unspeakable family tragedy, a devastating physical injury, and the potential loss of a lucrative financial career all happening simultaneously? While every person handles life's challenges differently, and professional assistance is often required, *Sports Illustrated*'s Greg Bishop profiled Prescott and gave us a picture into his inspirational journey in its September 15 edition.

First, Prescott gave thanks in the midst of circumstance. It sounds counterintuitive, but while lying on the field, Prescott remembered a friend telling him to thank God over and over in times of crisis. Even in the midst of tears streaming down his face, that is exactly what Prescott did. He said, "That (thanking God) was my peace in all of this." Prescott also focused on serving others. On the day of his injury, Prescott served his teammate, backup quarterback Andy Dalton, by texting him a congratulatory message on winning the game. He also served his family by texting his Aunt Gilbeaux, "Quit crying; I will be fine. It will be fine."

Even more astonishingly is how Prescott served others during his recovery. He raised money for cancer research in his mother's honor. Prescott also donated $1 million for police training and donated thousands of meals to the homeless. Furthermore, Prescott partnered with three mental health organizations. He sponsored various after-school programs and supported wrongly-accused and incarcerated Julius Jones. This is just a short list of his impact off the field in the lives of others.

It was also during the off-season that team owner Jerry Jones finally awarded Prescott with a well-deserved four-year contract extension worth $160 million. The quarterback would be the most high-profile player on the NFL's most high-profile team for the foreseeable future.

Through him, we learn what the leader's greatest strength is. Because of his background and other family tragedies not mentioned, Prescott possesses an uncommon mental toughness. He has a unique term for his approach to life saying, "What I've been through, I'll call it a *callused mind*. Just another scratch that'll heal up, that's make me stronger." What is required to develop a callused mind? Prescott reflected, "There's no way to put into words the fact that, yeah, the last time I was out there, I got my leg snapped, and there was a lot of uncertainty in the world. When you're doing so much, just being intentional and purposeful, it's amazing to get to do what you love to do again."

A callused mind requires focus, intentionality, and purposefulness. It has been said that hard times will make you bitter—or make you better. Prescott has clearly become better, and he's not done yet. He said, "I'm going to be a better player in every aspect. The things that have happened, they've allowed me to be here, but I don't even know if I've reaped the strength yet. What I mean is . . . that's to come."

It was then Prescott gave us his greatest strength: *"Perspective has become my greatest strength."*

November 24—Five Words a Leader Should Rarely (If Ever) Say

Dimorphos is a 530-foot asteroid orbiting in outer space. This week, NASA launched the fifty-nine-foot Double Asteroid Redirection Test (DART) out of California in hopes of slamming it into the asteroid and altering its course. Don't worry, we are not in trouble! No need to call Bruce Willis or stock up on toilet paper. Dimorphos was singled out and targeted for an experiment just in case an extinction-level threat was to ever occur. If the test is successful, DART will hit Dimorphos in September 2022 at a speed of 15,000 miles per hour.

A helpful exercise is to look at this experiment from the asteroid's point of view. What did Dimorphos ever do to deserve this? The asteroid is just minding its own business, going through space, and not hurting anyone or anything. Then suddenly—BANG— it is going to be blindsided by a spacecraft at 15,000 mph! Surely, the environmentalists must have a problem with this! But since Dimorphos is a giant rock with no capacity for pain or feelings, we don't even consider its point of view. Nor should we.

But what about leaders when they get blindsided? Oftentimes, they are also going quietly about their business and serving others with excellence when—BANG—they get blindsided! The five words a leader should rarely (if ever) say are, "I didn't see that coming." Muhammad Ali once said "It's not the hardest punch that knocks you out. It's the one you never see coming." Leaders, what knock us out are the things we never see coming. Some of the leadership items that can often blindside us are betrayal, health issues, marketplace fluctuations, employee issues, slumps, competition, technology, and family issues. Anyone with a spouse, children, or aging parents knows we are all one phone call away from our life changing forever.

Leaders are always going to be blindsided. It just comes with the territory. The key is to not be constantly blindsided. The following are ten things you can do to be proactive in your leadership.

1. Invest in people. They are your only appreciable asset.
2. Be a continual learner.
3. Adapt. Understand no one likes change but a baby. However, change is a constant that leaders must embrace.
4. Prioritize your time. Utilize the Paretto Principle. Spend 80 percent of your time on the top 20 percent of your responsibilities.
5. Prioritize your family. The greatest leadership begins at home.
6. Develop perspective. Have the discernment to know which things you have control over and which things you don't.
7. Be grateful. Do not take the positive things or relationships in your life for granted.
8. Be generous and make sure to save money for downturns in the economy and seasonal dips.
9. Eat right, exercise, and get regular check-ups to protect your health.
10. Be resilient and mentally tough. When life knocks you down, remember that getting knocked down is not failure. Staying down is.

Dimorphos is about to be blind-sided. You don't have to.

Leaders, there are always things that happen in our life that we do not see coming. Practice the ten items listed above, and next time, it may lessen the blow.

November 27–Four Things Needed for Your Great Ideas to Come to Life

The movie *Jurassic Park* has a famous scene where paleontologist Dr. Grant, played by Sam Neill, discovers dinosaurs can now be produced through genetic engineering. He then tells his cohorts, "I think we're out of a job." To which the wise-cracking Dr. Ian Malcolm, played by Jeff Goldblum, responds, "Don't you mean extinct?" What few people know is Malcolm's quote was not in the original script. It has been reported the quote originated from director Stephen Spielberg's on-set conversation with the movie's visual effects supervisor Phil Tippett. After watching an early CGI scene of a T-Rex chasing a herd of dinosaurs, Spielberg immediately knew computer-generated images would dramatically change special effects and the movie industry forever. He said to Tippett, "You're out of a job." Tippett replied, "Don't you mean extinct?" As producers overheard this conversation, they realized the exchange was perfect dialogue for movie itself. The rest, as they say, is cinematic history.

Here is the lesson all leaders can learn from this exchange: Great ideas come to life when great minds give great ideas to a great team who are willing to change and can then execute on those ideas. Let me explain.

There were a set of perfect conditions in place in the story above. If these conditions can be recreated in your current environment, you can see great ideas come to life as well. What are those conditions? First, great ideas often come from great minds. So have as many smart people around you as possible. Great ideas also come from a lot of good ideas. So collect as many as possible. Tippett's quote on extinction flowed from evaluating their previously shot scenes.

Furthermore, great ideas come to life when people are willing to change. Spielberg and the movie's producers were willing to change their already-excellent script. Finally, great ideas come to life when they are given to a great team to execute. This is important. Execution is where great ideas often go to die. Having a team of talented people like Jeff Goldblum is a must if you want to see your ideas come to life.

To repeat, great ideas come to life when great minds give great ideas to a great team who are willing to change and can then execute on those ideas. Do you have these conditions in place? If not, I would recommend redshirting your great ideas until you do.

December 1—Why So Many Leaders Do Not Have Winning Cultures

Seth Godin says culture can be boiled down to eleven words—"This is who we are and this is what we do." In John U. Bacon's excellent book, *Let Them Lead: Unexpected Lessons in Leadership from America's Worst High School Hockey Team,* he makes the following comments about why he was willing to apply for the head coaching job of the winless Ann Arbor Huron High School River Rats:

- "I wanted to build something with others, something that felt like family, something that could last."
- "I did want it—badly."
- "I wanted to save the program from leaving the Metro League, being demoted to club status, or disbanding altogether."
- "I wanted to turn the team around."
- "I wanted the coaches and players to build something special together."
- "I wanted them to want to do those things."

- "I wanted every one of them to feel that, as soon as they opened the door to our locker room."
- "I wanted them to walk through the hallways in the new T-shirts, sweats, and jerseys declaring who they were and what they stood for."
- "I wanted them to get emotional at the senior banquet, fighting back tears while saying goodbye to an experience that had stamped them forever."
- "I wanted those things, but I figured they were not the end itself, but would come as the byproducts of a bigger mission."
- "I wanted to be part of something they all wanted to be a part of too."
- "I wanted everyone to feel that we were accomplishing something bigger than just winning games."
- "I wanted to show the hockey world what a true team looked like every night, win or lose."
- "I wanted our locker room to be the center of our work, our headquarters, the fire in the middle of our base camp."
- "I wanted to lead a program I would have loved to have played for myself."

Did you notice a consistent theme in Bacon's words? Fifteen times he used the phrase "I wanted." He clearly knew who he was, what he wanted, and how to effectively communicate it.

After reading Bacon's words, you begin to realize why so many leaders do not have winning cultures. Many leaders simply do not know who they are and what they want. As a result, they certainly can't communicate it with conviction. These leaders willingly forego their convictions and desires for their preferred culture when faced with pressure from outside forces. I've seen a lack of clarity, limited options and money, pressure, indecisiveness, desire for comfort, and fear of conflict hijack many cultures leaders wished to create. When this happens, a losing or unhealthy culture is the result.

Successful soccer managers Roger Schmidt, Thomas Tuchel, Julian Nagelsmann, Ralph Hasenhüttl, and Jurgen Klopp have cited their main coaching influence as Ralf Rangnick. Recently, Rangnick spoke at a coaching symposium on what is necessary to become an elite manager. Read several of his comments and see if you notice a similar theme:

1. "What is the job of a futbol head coach, to have *a clear idea* of how my team should play."
2. "What they all (great coaches) have in common that *they exactly know* how this kind of futbol they want to play, what it looks like *they have in their brains,* the video of a perfect game. *They have it in their minds and on their minds* and the job of a futbol manager is to transform this idea of futbol into the heads, hearts, brains, veins of your players. Motivation for me is a transfer of belief, conviction, an idea of futbol."
3. "In order to do that (motivation) *you need to be aware* of what kind of futbol you really want to play."
4. "The idea needs to be *in your brains yourself first* in order to be able to educate, to teach, to develop your own team."
5. "This is what all the top coaches in Europe have in common."

These two great leaders give us a clear picture of the first step needed in creating a winning culture. They are very clear on who they are, what they think, what success looks like, and how to communicate it.

Are you?

December 4—What Defeats Talent Almost Every Single Time

In 1985, two college dropouts performed one of the most infamous art heists in history. After crawling through an air conditioning duct, these "amateur" burglars stole 124 artifacts from the National Museum of Archaeology in Mexico City. One of their prized acquisitions was a jade Mayan ruler death mask. After later being apprehended by authorities, the investigation uncovered the artifacts were almost traded for cocaine. This heist captured the imagination of the public. So much so, their efforts inspired the 2018 film *Museo*. So how did these inexperienced thieves pull off such a task?

While the two individuals lacked significant education and experience, they more than made up for it with preparation. Authorities discovered the burglars canvased the museum *over fifty times* prior to the theft. The leadership lesson we can all take from this historic heist is preparation almost always beats talent when talent isn't prepared. If you are facing an upcoming significant task or assignment, there are multiple benefits to being fully-prepared. Being fully-prepared gives you more confidence. You've done it over and over again. Being fully-prepared also lowers your stress and anxiety. There is less to worry about. You've made the mistakes in practice so therefore, you're less likely to make them in the game.

Being fully-prepared also improves your focus. You are more "locked in." Being fully-prepared reduces mistakes. You have a greater attention to detail. If you are looking for mastery, being fully-prepared allows you grow deeper in your skills. You will simply get better because you've practiced more. Being fully-prepared helps eliminate assumption. You take nothing for granted.

In addition, being fully-prepared makes you more efficient. You remove the non-essentials. Being fully-prepared creates a greater sense of ownership of the results. This is because you've invested so much time and resources. Being fully-prepared blossoms creativity. A common misconception is we need to think outside the box in order to be more creative. The opposite is true. Constraints improve creativity. Everyone has a box. This box represents your boundaries. Once identified, being fully-prepared shows you how to fill it.

Most importantly, being fully-prepared increases your odds of success. If two amateurs can pull off one of the greatest art heists in history because of their preparation, you can accomplish significant things through preparation as well.

December 6–The Disastrous Results of Leaders Chasing the Wrong Things

On Monday, November 22, in the town of Blackroot Pool, West Midlands, of the United Kingdom, an eleven-year-old Jack Russell terrier named Freddy got off his leash and began chasing a rabbit. As a former owner of a Jack Russell, I know from personal experience how determined these terriers can get. Freddy ultimately chased the rabbit down a literal rabbit hole. In fact, he went so far down the hole he got stuck approximately nine feet below ground. The pet's owner Richard Hill could hear the dog whimpering but could not reach him. Once darkness fell, Hill gave up hope of rescuing the animal and stopped his efforts.

The next morning he returned to the location and to his surprise, still heard Freddy's cries for help. It was at this point he called the West Midland Fire and Rescue Service. Utilizing a *What3Word* app, rescuers identified the dog's general location. They then used cameras and listening gear to pinpoint Freddy's whereabouts even further. Finally, they used equipment normally designed for earthquakes and building collapses to dig a six-feet by nine-feet trench.

After working for two hours, Freddy was able to sprint out of the hole and into his owner's arms. Hill then said, "I have to say a huge 'thank you' to the firefighters. They were just unbelievable . . . It was just incredible when he ran out of the hole after the rescue; it was just like nothing had happened."

While this is a heartwarming story, there are definite warnings here for leaders. First, we as leaders can also chase the wrong things. We all have our own set of rabbits in our lives. Our attention can be diverted from what should be primary to secondary issues. This may be the crazy idea no one supports which will yield little to no return. Perhaps it is an unwise investment. Often, ADD or "shiny object syndrome" can overtake us.

Next, this reckless use of time and resources can cause us to get stuck as well. Our behavior may result in our calendar or finances being tied up and not allowing us to take advantage of much more worthwhile opportunities which may arise. Momentum will be lost. Morale is lowered. Trust in our leadership suffers. And finally, unlike Richard Hill, we will not be afforded the opportunity to call emergency services to help us out. We will be trapped and must suffer the consequences of our decisions and actions. Worst of all, so will all of those who are on our team and are the unfortunate recipients of our ill-advised escapade.

Leaders, be careful what you chase. It may be wise to stay on the leash. You could get stuck in a hole you can't get out of.

December 7–The First Question a Leader Should Ask Those on Their Team

In 1977, Tom Moore was named wide receivers coach for the Pittsburgh Steelers. This was a potentially intimidating assignment for a new coach with his first professional assignment.

After all, the Steelers wide receivers were talented, two-time Super Bowl champions and featured future Hall of Famers Lynn Swann and John Stallworth. Both were already established stars with Swann being a previous Super Bowl's Most Valuable Player.

In the book *Super Bowl Blueprints: Hall Of Famers Reveal The Keys To Football's Greatest Dynasties*, Moore said Swann approached him and said, "Okay, I know you were a college coach and I'm going to help you if I can. Here's the deal, Tom: A player can make a lot of money in pro football and I want to make a lot of money. I want to play as long as I can. So, John Stallworth and I know how to catch the football. Teach us what we don't know."

Moore then asked a great question. He asked, "Okay, what don't you know?"

Swann responded, "We don't have a clue how to adjust routes, how to read coverage, how to get open."

At that summer's training camp, Moore would spend the majority of his time coaching his receivers how to beat double coverages.

Throughout Moore's five subsequent decades in pro coaching, he would always tell his assistants, "When you go into your first meetings in OTAs, the first thing you have to do is take all your players and find out from them what they don't know, what they need work on, because they're not going to tell you unless you ask them. And if you ask them, that'll loosen them up and they'll feel free to tell you."

As leaders, we must understand your top talent want to be coached. Lynn Swann approached Tom Moore, not the other way around. Great players, great salespeople, great teachers, great pastors, great doctors and lawyers, etc . . . , they all want to get better. They want to be coached. Your most talented people become frustrated when they are not coached. The best of the best are truly committed to personal growth and will seek out opportunities to improve.

Also, wisdom comes from great questions, not great answers. Did not you notice Coach Moore did not say, "Lynn, I've been watching film and let me tell you what I'm seeing." No, he started by asking, "What don't you know?" He did not assume he knew Swann's deficiencies. Moore wanted to hear Swann's self-evaluation. Smart leaders never rush into situations with answers, but rather questions.

Asking great questions also uncovers a person's motivations. For Swann and Stallworth, it was to have a longer career and make more money.

Performance consultant Lewis Preston once taught me that top talent almost always self-corrects. You don't have to alert top talent to their deficiencies, they already know them and usually have a plan to self-correct. Swann's plan involved seeking out coaching. You only have to spend time pointing out deficiencies to your non-performers.

This brings me to the importance of efficiency. People are your most valuable resource. Time is second because when it's gone, you can't get it back. Once the improvement plan was identified, Coach Moore spent the majority of training camp working on that area. He did not focus his or his team's efforts on non-essentials. Practice is designed to help you get better. Therefore, they spent their time on the areas of improvement Swann had identified.

Moore said asking "What don't you know?' will 'loosen them up.'" Once again, one of the things which makes someone a top talent is their response to coaching and desire to get better. Many high achievers are initially standoffish but when you engage them with a desire to help them get better (and in this case, to have a longer career and increase their earning potential), it builds trust and creates a relational bridge.

Because Lynn Swann approached Tom Moore in the summer of 1977 with a performance improvement plan, Moore has since taught this approach to the hundreds of assistant coaches he has come in contact with over the last five decades. The number of players and the amount of improvement which has taken place because he trained them to ask, "What don't you know?" cannot be measured.

When you have your first meeting with your team or you want to improve performance, don't lead with suggestions or assumption. Start the conversation with a great question. Ask "What don't you know?" Their answer will also help make you a better leader.

December 16–*Spider-Man: No Way Home*

This movie is ultimately about a series of hard decisions made by Peter Parker—asking Dr. Strange for a spell, attempting to heal the villains rather than sending them back to their universe to die, and most of all, giving up all his personal relationships to save the planet. Leaders who aren't willing to sacrifice cease to be leaders.

That being said, smart leaders don't live in the past but they certainly touch it before moving forward. The inclusion of previous Sony Spider-Man characters results in some of the most memorable scenes in movie history. The interplay between Andrew Garfield and Tobey Maguire was surprising, delightful, and Oscar worthy. The theater I was in had loud cheers when they appeared on screen. In addition, you cannot overstate how much Marvel honored their audience in this movie by bringing them back.

Another lesson from the movie was teamwork makes the dream work. During the climatic battle scene, two of the three Spider-Men (I can't believe I just typed that sentence) realized they had never worked in a team setting before. They always operated individually. However, to defeat five super-villains they had to work together. Tom Holland's Spider-Man referred to his Avengers experience and showed them how to work as a team.

Finally, successful leaders know everyone deserves a second chance. In fact, "everyone deserves a second chance" was one of Aunt Mae's favorite sayings and a constant theme throughout the movie. Nowhere was this highlighted more than when Garfield's Spider-Man had a chance to save MJ, thus giving him redemption for the death of Gwen Stacy in a previous film.

But the most important leadership lesson of the movie was Aunt Mae's final words to Parker, "With great power comes great responsibility." Leaders have a high and holy calling. It is a great responsibility to help people reach their full potential and their organization see their mission and vision realized.

Leadership is not something to be entered into lightly. It is full of hard decisions.

December 18—What Steph Curry Teaches Us About Being Unappreciated, Dismissed, and Marginalized

On Tuesday, December 14 with 7:33 remaining in the first quarter of the team's game against the New York Knicks, Golden State Warriors incomparable point guard Steph Curry broke Ray Allen's all-time 3-point field goal record of 2,973.

To understand the impact of this record on the game of basketball, consider the following provided by the daily sports newsletter Sideline Sprint:

- In 2009, the number of three-point shots attempted league wide was 44,583 (22% of all shots). In 2020, the number shot to 74,822 (39% of all shots).
- Steph has the most games with 9+ threes in NBA history (40). The rest of the NBA combined has 39.
- Steph has averaged 5+ threes per game in a season four times. The rest of the NBA has never done that—even James Harden maxed out at 4.8.
- It took Steph 789 games to break Ray Allen's record, which took Allen 1,300 games to set.

But more than his impact on the game, Curry inspires everyone who has ever felt under-sized, unappreciated, overlooked, and marginalized to achieve great things and not settle for less in their lives anymore.

Steph's father Dell said, "In Chicago the other day, I saw LaVar Ball at the game wearing a hat that said: 'I Told You So.' Well, my hat would say: 'I Had No Idea.'" No one did. Steph was a 3-star recruit, considered the #52 high school *point guard* (not player, point guard!) in the country, and attended Davidson after being turned down by all the top college programs.

But Curry harnessed his inner-drive, high-character, hard work, focus, repetition, and a positive attitude into developing an elite skill which is in high-demand—shooting a basketball. And he did so at a level no one had ever achieved before. Curry would become the greatest shooter in basketball history.

The lesson for all of us is that while we may not become the greatest basketball shooter of all-time, we can certainly accomplish great things in our own lives as well. And don't ever let anyone tell you that you can't.

Others may dismiss us because of our background, education, appearance, ethnicity, or some other subjective parameter. In fact, we may even dismiss ourselves. But when we are people of high-character with a positive attitude, who work hard, focus our efforts, and do it consistently over a long period of time, we too can accomplish great things.

Steph Curry has given countless people permission to not accept a sub-standard life anymore. We too can achieve great things and are now without excuse. There is nothing stopping us—just our own decision to listen to the naysayers and not consistently put in the work needed to achieve excellence in our lives.

December 19–Snoasis

On Friday, November 26, 2021 the band Noasis, a tribute band for the group Oasis, performed at the Tan Hill Inn in Richmond, England. While entertaining those in attendance, a snowstorm descended on this city located 200 miles northwest of London.

So much snow fell that approximately 60 patrons, employees, and band members were trapped in the Inn for three days! Some children and a man with a medical condition were evacuated but everyone else hunkered down for a memorable time together in something now known as Snoasis.

Those stranded kept themselves busy with karaoke, games, more music from the band, and a tremendous amount of food and adult beverages.

When the weather cleared and everyone was able to leave the following Monday, the Inn posted on its Facebook page, "We will ALWAYS remember this group of amazing people who came together, and hopefully, in challenging circumstances, enjoyed what we all think was a life—changing experience."

Snoasis teaches us several things.

First, is the power of perspective. Many people reading this post would think those stranded would develop "cabin fever" or go through other various forms of anger or anxiety. While that would certainly be understandable, those in attendance chose to enjoy what was right in front of them. Rather than looking at the negative, they chose to enjoy the extra time with friends and the band they love, warm housing, and plenty of good food and drink

This speaks to their positive attitude. Think about it, is there anything leaders hate more than inconvenience and inefficiency? While I may not have experienced anxiousness being snowed in, I certainly would have been annoyed. After all, I've got things planned for the weekend. I've got things to do. In fact, why did I ever come to this in the first place since it was snowing? And because I approach things this way, my negative attitude would have caused me to miss out on one of the most memorable events of my life.

My attitude would have disqualified me from having a wonderful memory.

A positive attitude opens up your heart and mind to possibilities. Positive people are simply more attractive and enjoyable to be around. A positive attitude makes you more "lucky." Those in attendance had an incredible three days. I wonder if I would have.

People need to do a better job embracing life's inconveniences. It is at the edge of uncomfortable where greatness resides. Who knew being trapped in a snowstorm would garner worldwide attention for those in attendance? Blessings often come disguised as unexpected detours and inconveniences. Embrace them.

I'm convinced one of the reasons people were so willing to shelter-in-place was their collective appreciation of the band Noasis. They got the privilege of spending three extra days with the band they love and get to know them personally! The success of any band, artist, business, political candidate, or church is their ability to grow a passionate group of followers who become the organization's evangelists. Noasis certainly has.

While not discussed, the ability of the Inn's staff to adapt and pivot during the snowstorm cannot be overstated. People are a picture of those in leadership. The staff clearly thought of various contingencies to handle the snow, power, food, beverages, housing, and all other needs to care for those who were stranded. This was an A+ effort by those employees.

There have been discussions about making Snoasis an annual event for those who were stranded. I know if I'm in Richmond, England, I'll be there. . . . and ready to stay for several days if needed.

December 22–Two Extraordinary Acts Of Generosity

It is easy to become depressed or cynical about things in the world today. But there are always inspirational rays of hope if you are willing to look for them.

Recently, I discovered two stories of generosity which I think will inspire you.

In 2017, the University of Iowa Stead Family Children's Hospital opened. It sits just adjacent to the school's football stadium. During games, the hospital's patients and their families would begin watching the action from their windows. In response, a beautiful tradition was born.

At the end of the first quarter, the players and 70,000 people in attendance would focus their attention away from the game and onto the hospital's children and begin waving to them. Few things are as heartwarming. So much so, opposing teams now waive to the children as well.

On December 17th, the team's center Tyler Linderbaum took it a step farther. He donated his $30,000 Name Image Likeness (NIL) earnings to the children's hospital.

Many people think NIL will ruin college sports. No doubt, it will certainly change it. But similar to things like the internet, social media, and money, college athletes can now use their earnings for good or for bad. Linderbaum provides an example of what can happen when you combine a generous spirit with NIL earnings. It can do a lot of good in the world.

Second story. Which sports team, regardless of where it is in the world, has the best fan base? Could it be the Green Bay Packers? Pittsburgh Steelers? New York Yankees? Boston Red Sox? Auburn or Alabama? Any number of European or Brazilian soccer teams? How about the All Blacks rugby team?

There are dozens of passionate fan bases across the globe but fans of the Buffalo Bills, known as the Bills Mafia, recently made a compelling case for why they should be at the top of the list.

Tre'Davious White is a 5th year cornerback for the team. The former first-round pick out of LSU is a two-time All-Pro and tied for the league lead in interceptions in 2019. He is not only one of the team's best players, but one of the best in the NFL.

On November 25th in a game against the New Orleans Saints, White suffered a season-ending knee injury. It was then the Bills Mafia stepped up.

White's uniform number is 27. A group of Bills' fans began making $27 donations to the Food Bank of Northwest Louisiana in his honor. Think about that, Shreveport, La, the food bank's location, is 1,260 miles from Buffalo, NY. The level of insight, care, compassion, creativity, and generosity of this fan base is extraordinary!

So what were the results?

As of December 1st, over $108,000 had been received!!!

The food bank's executive director Martha Marak said, "We appreciate Tre'Davious White's generosity and all he gives back to our community. We are so honored to have the support from the Bills Mafia Babes. These donations come at a time when food insecurity for our neighbors is high and our food inventory is low. With the food bank's resources, we will turn every $1 donated into $10 in food value and every $27 that is donated allows us to provide food for 100 meals. As it stands currently, the donations will provide $1,083,590 worth of food value—a number we are so grateful for. We look forward to continuing the fight to end hunger together."

There are a number of wonderful fan bases. Until I hear a story which tops this act of generosity, I'm going with the Bills Mafia as the most passionate. . . . and most generous fan base in the world.

I hope these stories inspired you and maybe, just maybe, perhaps inspired you to be a little more generous as well.

December 25–Achieving Mastery In 2022

I want to close 2021 out by discussing what it will require of you as a leader to achieve mastery in your task or assignment in 2022.

On July 4, 2016 superstar forward Kevin Durant announced he was joining the 73-win and Western Conference champion Golden State Warriors. In an absurdity of riches, Durant joined two-time Most Valuable Player Steph Curry and Klay Thompson to give the team perhaps the three greatest shooters of all-time.

The Warriors would go on to win the next two NBA titles with relative ease. When discussions take place about the greatest teams in game's history, the 2016–18 Warriors are at or the near the top of the conversation.

The team's head coach Steve Kerr was once asked what it was like coaching the team's superstars. He said, "I watch Kevin Durant and Steph Curry and Klay Thompson everyday work on their shooting at the end of practice, and I just marvel at the attention to detail. Each guy has their own routine, and when we finish practice, they each go to their own basket, with their own coach, who goes through their routine with them."

He then adds, "It's every single day. They are pushing themselves and pushing each other. When you think, these are possibly the three best shooters on earth and here they are working on their craft, every single day with such precision and such dedication, that's mastery."

One desire all leaders have (or should have) is to achieve mastery in their area of influence. From Kerr's comments, we learn five things which are required to do so.

To achieve mastery you put in the extra work. Unfortunately, many people only put in the minimum amount required to do their job. These individuals will never achieve mastery because they don't put in the lonely work no one sees.

Durant, Curry, and Thompson practiced hard. They put in the work required. But as talented as they were, they went a step further and put in extra work after practice.

To achieve mastery you must also have great attention to detail. Mastery requires precision. There should be no wasted energy. Masters have learned to edit their life and remove all non-essentials. They only focus on that which takes them in the direction of their desired destination.

Individuals who have mastered their craft also have consistency and a system. Proverbs 21:5 says, "The plans of the diligent lead to harvest, as sure as haste leads to poverty." (NIV). There are two components to this lesson, a plan and diligence. You cannot achieve mastery without both. The three players mentioned had "their own routine" and put in the work "every single day."

In addition, rarely can you achieve mastery alone. Everyone gets better with a coach. The three greatest shooters in NBA history had individual coaches. Tiger Woods had a swing coach. Tom Brady has a personal coach. Presidents have speech writers. Get the point. Whatever profession you are in, you will never achieve mastery without getting the right coach to help you.

Finally, to achieve mastery you need a rival who will push you beyond your current capacity. There needs to a person or organization which pushes you every day to get better. Masters of their craft are inherently competitive. As Curry, Durant, and Thompson competed with one another in practice, the weight room, film work, nutrition, rest, and being a good teammate, none were going to let someone else get the better of them. And they made each other the best they could be.

Having a rival in your company or industry is not a bad thing, it's a gift.

In conclusion, if these five things are in place in 2022, you have a chance to achieve mastery in your field.

December 31–Conclusion

Craig Groeschel once said, "A great leader also plans for unexpected opportunities. Wherever there is uncertainty, there is always opportunity. The most significant and impactful things we've ever done were born in uncertain times and we never planned for them to do."

Undoubtedly, 2021 was a year of great uncertainty. We were coming off a year which will live in infamy. 2020 was a year of political unrest, social instability, economic disruption, and health crises. But as Craig said, out of great uncertainty comes great opportunity.

My desire is the stories and principles you have read in the previous pages will serve as a guide for how to move forward and better influence others.

John Maxwell famously said, "Everything rises and falls on leadership." John was right.

And here is what I know about you, God never wastes experience. Because you have taken the time to read this book, God will use its countless lessons to make you a better leader and when a leader gets better, everyone wins. And everything rises.

It has been a privilege to help you win. Please subscribe to Brian Dodd On Leadership and I will continue investing in your leadership throughout the following year.

God bless.

About the Author

Brian Dodd is the Director of New Ministry Partnerships for INJOY Stewardship Solutions. Over the last two decades, he has had countless conversations with thousands of leaders in both the profit and non-profit space.

He is the author of *Timeless: 10 Enduring Practices Of Apex Leaders* and *The 2-Minute Leader*. From this he created the popular 11-module 2-Minute Leader Coaching Course. But what Brian is most known for is his uber-popular Brian Dodd On Leadership website which is one the most read Christian leadership sites in the world.

Brian has been featured on countless national podcasts and publications. In addition, he has been recognized as one of *Inc. Magazine* Top 100 speakers on leadership. You can hear Brian along with his cohost Jeff Wright on the popular *Pursuit Of Service* Podcast where they discuss real-time leadership issues.

He and his wife, Sonya, have been married for over 30 years, and they have one daughter, Anna. Brian is actively involved at Piedmont Church in Marietta, GA where Sonya serves on staff.

2021: The Year In Leadership Bibliography

Handling Tragedy and Setbacks—Pages 18–19
Will Buxton, **My Greatest Defeat: Stories of hardship and hope from motor racing's finest heroes (Evro Publishing, 2019), 29–47.**

Changing a Losing Culture into a Winning One—Pages 19–20
Sam Khan Jr., "How Matt Campbell turned around Iowa State football," January 2, 2021, https://www.espn.com/college-football/story/_/id/30633499/how-matt-campbell-turned-iowa-state-football

Signs Pastors Do Not Respect Their Elder Board—Pages 37–38
English Standard Version is used for these pages.

Five Things We Must Communicate for a Sermon or Speech to Be Effective—Pages 39–40
English Standard Version is used for these pages.

Why Great Organizations, Teams, and People Are Destroyed from Within—Pages 42–43
Ethan Sherwood Strauss, *The Victory Machine: The Making and Unmaking of the Warriors Dynasty* (Hatchett Book Group, Inc., 2020)

The Glue That Holds Teams Together—Pages 45–46
Buster Olney, *The Last Night of the Yankee Dynasty: The Game, the Team, and the Cost of Greatness* (Ecco, HarperCollins Publishers, 2004), 264.

Eight Keys to Have Sustainable Organizational Success—Pages 47–48
Tim Kawakami, *The Athletic*, "Kyle Shanahan and John Lynch's long-term 49ers stability, and what that means for Julio Jones" June 2, 2021. https://theathletic.com/2618552/2021/06/02/49ers-julio-jones-kyle-shanahan-john-lynch/

Father's Day—Pages 52–53
New International Version is used for these pages.

Nick Saban on Reinforcing the Values of the Organization—Page 53
Joe Smith, *The Athletic*, "Champions culture: Real or overhyped? Coaching titans Kerr, Maddon, Arians, and Saban weigh in." June 24, 2021. https://theathletic.com/2647150/2021/06/24/championship-culture-real-or-overhyped-coaching-titans-kerr-maddon-arians-and-saban-weigh-in/

Sir Alex Ferguson—Pages 53–54
Simon Kuper, *Soccer Men: Profiles of the Rogues, Geniuses, and Neurotics Who Dominate the World's Most Popular Sport* (Nations Books, 2011, 2014), 296–298.

Shohei Ohtani—Pages 54–56
Rustin Dodd, *The Athletic*, "Shohei Ohtani is 'in his own world' . . . which appears to be somewhere beyond baseball's outer limits," June 30, 2021, https://theathletic.com/2665880/2021/06/30/shohei-ohtani-is-in-his-own-world-which-appears-to-be-somewhere-beyond-baseballs-outer-limits/?source=dailyemail

Chris Paul—Pages 58–59
Jovan Buha, *The Athletic*, "Chris Paul's leadership has evolved with Suns: 'It's only leadership if people follow you,'" July 6, 2021, https://theathletic.com/2690467/2021/07/06/

chris-pauls-leadership-has-evolved-with-suns-its-only-leader-ship-if-people-follow-you/

Solo Cups—Pages 59–60
Matty Merritt, *Morning Brew,* "Origin Stories: July Fourth's Favorite Companies," July 2, 2021, https://www.morningbrew.com/daily/stories/2021/07/02/origin-stories-july-fourths-favorite-companies

Twenty Questions to Determine Pastoral Trust—Page 62
English Standard Version is used for these pages.

Nick Saban's Eight Benefits to Being on a Team—Page 67
Sam Kahn, Jr., *The Athletic,* "Nick Saban opens up to Texas high school coaches on Drew Brees, those Texas rumors and why 'you adapt or die,'" July 20, 2021, https://theathletic.com/2718738/2021/07/20/nick-saban-opens-up-to-texas-high-school-coaches-on-drew-brees-those-texas-rumors-and-why-you-adapt-or-die/?source=weeklyemail

Alaskan Bear Attack—Pages 67–69
Alexander Haro, *The Inertia,* "Grizzly Bear Attacks Man at a Remote Mining Claim in Alaska; Stalk Him for a Week Straight," July 25, 2021, https://www.theinertia.com/news/grizzly-bear-attack-alaska-mining-claim-man-stalked/

The Inner-Circle—Pages 69–70
English Standard Version is used for these pages.

Who Is Responsible for Maintaining Culture in Your Organization?—Pages 70–71
Kunal Sethi, *sportskeeda,* "'It's on me to maintain that culture'— Stephen Curry talks about staying with Golden State Warriors for the rest of his career," August 4, 2021, https://www.sportskeeda.

com/basketball/news-it-s-maintain-culture-stephen-curry-talks-staying-golden-state-warriors-rest-career

What If?—Pages 73–74
Francesca Gina, *Rebel Talent: Why It Pays To Break the Rules at Work and Life* (Harper Collins, 2018), 63–64.

The Number 1 Asset Leaders Have for Problem Solving—Pages 75–76
English Standard Version is used for these pages.

Smart Decisions and Bad Decisions—Pages 76–78
Wikipedia (Ferruccio Lamborghini). https://en.wikipedia.org/wiki/Ferruccio_Lamborghini

Stray Cat Falls from Upper Deck—Pages 78–79
https://www.youtube.com/watch?v=C3Ds7BxAMxE

The Questions Your Organization Should Be Asking—Pages 81–82
Jeremy Gutsche, *Create The Future: Tactics For Disruptive Thinking,* (Fast Company Press, 2020), 2–5

The Thing Most Leaders Are Missing—Pages 82–84
Simon Kuper, *The Barcelona Complex: Lionel Messi and the Making—and Unmaking—of the World's Greatest Soccer Club,* (Penguin Press, 2021), 288–289;
Jeremy Gutsche, *Create The Future: Tactics For Disruptive Thinking,* (Fast Company Press, 2020), 163.

Not Knowing What Business You Are Truly In—Pages 85–87
Andrea Nagy Smith, *Yale Insights,* "What Was Polaroid Thinking," November 4, 2009, https://insights.som.yale.edu/insights/what-was-polaroid-thinking;

Jeremy Gutsche, *Create the Future: Tactics for Disruptive Thinking*, (Fast Company Press, 2020), 168;

John Maxwell, *The 21 Irrefutable Laws of Leadership: Follow Them and People Will Follow You*, (Maxwell Motivation, Inc., Thomas Nelson, 1998), 175

How to Know When a Leader Trusts You—Pages 88–90
"The Brady 6," NFL Films, https://www.youtube.com/watch?v=o5fdhfVrg1I

How Dabo Swinney Gets Big Financial Gifts from Wealthy People—Pages 90–91
King James Version is used for these pages.
Lars Anderson, *Dabo's World: The Life and Career of Coach Swinney and the Rise of Clemson Football*, (Hatchette Book Group, Inc, 2021), 149–150.

The One Thing the Greatest Leaders Do (Which Others Don't) to Become Successful—Pages 91–92
Greg Cosell, *The 33rd Team*, "What Makes A Quarterback Successful," October 22, 2021, https://www.the33rdteam.com/what-makes-a-quarterback-successful/

Can One Person Change an Organization's Culture—Pages 96–98
Lars Anderson, *A Season in the Sun: The Inside Story of Bruce Arians, Tom Brady, and the Making of a Champion*, (Harper Collins, 2021)

Foo Fighters Lead Singer David Grohl's Remarkable Interactions with a Special Needs Fan—Pages 98–100
Twitter, @Todd_Spencer, November 7, 2021

You Can't Lead Anyone Unless You Do This First—Pages 100–101
Umamaheswaran Dhananjayan, *"The famous Ghandi sugar story,"* October 16, 2019, https://www.linkedin.com/pulse/famous-gandhi-sugar-story-umamaheswaran-dhananjayan?trk=related_artice_The%20famous%20Gandhi%20sugar%20story_article-card_title

40 Things Average People Don't Do—Pages 103–104
Tim Elmore, *The Eight Paradoxes of Great Leadership: Embracing the Conflicting Demands of Today's Workplace,* (Harper Collins Leadership, 2021), 164.

A Leader's Greatest Strength—Pages 107–108
Greg Bishop, *Sports Illustrated,* September 15, 2021.

Five Words a Leader Should Rarely (If Ever) Say—Pages 108–109
Paul Rincon, *bbc.com,* "Nasa Dart asteroid spacecraft: Mission to smash into Dimorphos space rock launches," November 24, 2021, https://www.bbc.com/news/science-environment-59327293

Four Things Needed for Your Great Ideas Come to Life—Page 110
Jasper Drake, *cheatsheet.com,* "'Jurassic Park': 1 of Jeff Goldblum's Iconic Lines Happened By Accident, January 16, 2021, https://www.cheatsheet.com/entertainment/jurassic-park-1-of-jeff-goldblums-iconic-lines-happened-by-accident.html/

Why So Many Leaders Do Not Have Winning Cultures—Pages 111–112
John U. Bacon, *Let Them Lead: Unexpected Lessons in Leadership from America's Worst High School Hockey Team,* (Houghton Mifflin Harcourt Publishing Company, 2021), 7–9; https://www.youtube.com/watch?v=EJ7zEahtgpA

What Defeats Talent Almost Every Single Time—Pages 112–113
Alex Greenberger, *artnews.com*, "The 25 Greatest Art Heists of All Time," February 11, 2021, https://www.artnews.com/list/art-news/artists/greatest-art-heists-of-all-time-1234583441/

The Disastrous Results of Leaders Chasing the Wrong Things—Pages 113–114
Good News Network, *goodnewsnetwork.org*, "Firefighters Rescue a Dog Trapped Down a 15-Foot Underground Burrow Overnight," November 27, 2021, https://www.goodnewsnetwork.org/dog-freed-from-rabbit-hole-by-disaster-rescue-equipment/

The First Question a Leader Should Ask Those on Their Team—Pages 114–116
Bill Polian and Vic Carucci, *Super Bowl Blueprints: Hall of Famers Reveal the Keys to Football's Greatest Dynasties,* (Triumph Books LLC, 2021), 74.

Snoasis—Pages 118–119
The Tan Hill Inn Facebook post, November 26, 2021.

Two Extraordinary Acts of Generosity—Pages 119–120
https://www.youtube.com/watch?v=yObg1JTIx5M
Chris Vannini Twitter, December 19, 2021

Achieving Mastery in 2022—Pages 120–121
New International Version is used for these pages.